First World War
and Army of Occupation
War Diary
France, Belgium and Germany

2 DIVISION
Divisional Troops
Royal Army Medical Corps
4 Field Ambulance
1 March 1915 - 31 March 1915

WO95/1336/3

The Naval & Military Press Ltd
www.nmarchive.com
Published in association with The National Archives

Published by

The Naval & Military Press Ltd

Unit 10 Ridgewood Industrial Park,

Uckfield, East Sussex,

TN22 5QE England

Tel: +44 (0) 1825 749494

www.naval-military-press.com

www.nmarchive.com

This diary has been reprinted in facsimile from the original. Any imperfections are inevitably reproduced and the quality may fall short of modern type and cartographic standards.

Contents

Document type	Place/Title	Date From	Date To
Heading	March 1915 No.4 Field Ambulance Vol VIII		
War Diary	Bethune	01/03/1915	31/03/1915
Miscellaneous	4 Field Ambulance		
Miscellaneous	No.4 Field Ambulance Evacuation Return	01/03/1915	01/03/1915
Miscellaneous	No.4 Field Ambulance Evacuation Return	02/03/1915	02/03/1915
Miscellaneous	No.4 Field Ambulance Evacuation Return	03/03/1915	03/03/1915
Miscellaneous	No.4 Field Ambulance Evacuation Return	04/03/1915	04/03/1915
Miscellaneous	Evacuation Return	05/03/1915	05/03/1915
Miscellaneous	No.4 Field Ambulance Evacuation Return	05/03/1915	05/03/1915
Miscellaneous	No.4 Field Ambulance Evacuation Return	06/03/1915	06/03/1915
Miscellaneous	No.4 Field Ambulance Evacuation Return	07/03/1915	07/03/1915
Miscellaneous	No.4 Field Ambulance Evacuation Return	08/03/1915	08/03/1915
Miscellaneous	No.4 Field Ambulance Evacuation Return	09/03/1915	09/03/1915
Miscellaneous	Evacuation Return	10/03/1915	10/03/1915
Miscellaneous	No. 4 Motor Convoy Evacuation Return	10/03/1915	10/03/1915
Miscellaneous	No. 4 Motor Convoy Evacuation Return	11/03/1915	11/03/1915
Miscellaneous	No. 4 Motor Convoy Evacuation Return	12/03/1915	12/03/1915
Miscellaneous	No.4 Field Ambulance Evacuation Return	12/03/1915	12/03/1915
Miscellaneous	No.4 Field Ambulance Evacuation Return	13/03/1915	13/03/1915
Miscellaneous	No.4 Field Ambulance Evacuation Return	14/03/1915	14/03/1915
Miscellaneous	No.4 Field Ambulance Evacuation Return	15/03/1915	15/03/1915
Miscellaneous	No.4 Field Ambulance Evacuation Return	16/03/1915	16/03/1915
Miscellaneous	No.4 Field Ambulance Evacuation Return	17/03/1915	17/03/1915
Miscellaneous	No.4 Field Ambulance Evacuation Return	18/03/1915	18/03/1915
Miscellaneous	No.4 Field Ambulance Evacuation Return	19/03/1915	19/03/1915
Miscellaneous	No.4 Field Ambulance Evacuation Return	20/03/1915	20/03/1915
Miscellaneous	No.4 Field Ambulance Evacuation Return	21/03/1915	21/03/1915
Miscellaneous	No.4 Field Ambulance Evacuation Return		
Miscellaneous	No.4 Field Ambulance Evacuation Return	23/03/1915	23/03/1915
Miscellaneous	No.4 Field Ambulance Evacuation Return	24/03/1915	24/03/1915
Miscellaneous	No.4 Field Ambulance Evacuation Return	25/03/1915	25/03/1915
Miscellaneous	No.4 Field Ambulance Evacuation Return	26/03/1915	26/03/1915
Miscellaneous	No.4 Field Ambulance Evacuation Return	28/03/1915	28/03/1915
Miscellaneous	No.4 Field Ambulance Evacuation Return	29/03/1915	29/03/1915
Miscellaneous	No.4 Field Ambulance Evacuation Return	30/03/1915	30/03/1915
Miscellaneous	No.4 Field Ambulance Evacuation Return	31/03/1915	31/03/1915
Miscellaneous	No.4 Field Ambulance Table Showing No of Sick Wounded	01/03/1915	01/03/1915
Miscellaneous	No.4 Field Ambulance Table Shewing No of Sick Wounded	02/03/1915	02/03/1915
Miscellaneous	No.4 Field Ambulance Table Showing No of Sick Wounded	04/03/1915	04/03/1915
Miscellaneous	No.4 Field Ambulance Table Showing No of Sick Wounded	05/03/1915	05/03/1915
Miscellaneous	No.4 Field Ambulance Table Showing No of Sick Wounded	04/03/1915	04/03/1915
Miscellaneous	No.4 Field Ambulance Table Showing No of Sick Wounded	07/03/1915	07/03/1915
Miscellaneous	No.4 Field Ambulance Table Showing No of Sick Wounded	08/03/1915	08/03/1915

Miscellaneous	No.4 Field Ambulance Table Showing No of Sick Wounded	09/03/1915	09/03/1915
Miscellaneous	No.4 Field Ambulance Table Showing No of Sick Wounded	11/03/1915	11/03/1915
Miscellaneous	Nominal Roll of Officer Admitted	11/03/1915	11/03/1915
Miscellaneous	No. 4 Field Ambulance Table Shewing No of Sick Wounded	12/03/1915	12/03/1915
Miscellaneous	No. 4 Field Ambulance Table Showing No of Sick Wounded	13/03/1915	13/03/1915
Miscellaneous	No. 4 Field Ambulance Table Showing No of Sick Wounded	14/03/1915	14/03/1915
Miscellaneous	No. 4 Field Ambulance Table Showing No of Sick Wounded	15/03/1915	15/03/1915
Miscellaneous	No. 4 Field Ambulance Table Showing No of Sick Wounded	16/03/1915	16/03/1915
Miscellaneous	No. 4 Field Ambulance Table Showing No of Sick Wounded	17/03/1915	17/03/1915
Miscellaneous	No. 4 Field Ambulance Table Showing No of Sick Wounded	18/03/1915	18/03/1915
Miscellaneous	No. 4 Field Ambulance Table Showing No of Sick Wounded	19/03/1915	19/03/1915
Miscellaneous	No. 4 Field Ambulance Table Showing No of Sick Wounded	20/03/1915	20/03/1915
Miscellaneous	No. 4 Field Ambulance Table Showing No of Sick Wounded	21/03/1915	21/03/1915
Miscellaneous	No. 4 Field Ambulance Table Showing No of Sick Wounded	22/03/1915	22/03/1915
Miscellaneous	No. 4 Field Ambulance Table Showing No of Sick Wounded	23/03/1915	23/03/1915
Miscellaneous	No. 4 Field Ambulance Table Showing No of Sick Wounded	24/03/1915	24/03/1915
Miscellaneous	No. 4 Field Ambulance Table Showing No of Sick Wounded	25/03/1915	25/03/1915
Miscellaneous	No. 4 Field Ambulance Table Showing No of Sick Wounded	26/03/1915	26/03/1915
Miscellaneous	No. 4 Field Ambulance Table Showing No of Sick Wounded	27/03/1915	27/03/1915
Miscellaneous	No. 4 Field Ambulance Table Showing No of Sick Wounded	28/03/1915	28/03/1915
Miscellaneous	No. 4 Field Ambulance Table Showing No of Sick Wounded	29/03/1915	29/03/1915
Miscellaneous	No. 4 Field Ambulance Table Showing No of Sick Wounded	30/03/1915	30/03/1915
Miscellaneous	No. 4 Field Ambulance Table Showing No of Sick Wounded	31/03/1915	31/03/1915
Heading	Operations In March		

March 1915

121/4846

S

No 4. Field Ambulance

Vol VIII

No. 4 F. A. Mar 1915.

Plan of Portion of Civil & Military Hpl - Bethune, has been detached & filed under "Plans, maps etc."

Instructions regarding War Diaries and Intelligence Summaries are contained in F. S. Regs., Part II. and the Staff Manual respectively. Title pages will be prepared in manuscript.

WAR DIARY
or
~~INTELLIGENCE~~ SUMMARY.
(Erase heading not required.)

Hour, Date, Place	Summary of Events and Information
March 1st/15 BETHUNE	Capt W W Boyce RAMC } proceeded Lieut Wm H. McCullagh } on leave ADMS. 2 Division inspected the Officers Dressing station Brigadier Genl. H C Lowther 1st Brigade 1st Division admitted to Officers Dressing station. N.Y.D. Brigadier General the Earl of Cavan admitted suffering from Influenza No of Casualties – 39. Lt. R. Crane. Shell Wnd. Head. } evacuated R.G.A. } by M.A.C. 2nd Lt. A. Silcock 2 Sth Staffs No 2749 PERCIVAL. J. 3rd Coldstream Gds retd to a[illegible] with 3rd Coldstream Gds.

(73989) W4141—463. 400,000. 9/14. H.&J.Ltd. Forms/C. 2118/10.

Instructions regarding War Diaries and Intelligence Summaries are contained in F. S. Regs., Part II. and the Staff Manual respectively. Title pages will be prepared in manuscript.

WAR DIARY
or
~~INTELLIGENCE~~ SUMMARY.
(Erase heading not required.)

Army Form C. 2118.

Hour, Date, Place	Summary of Events and Information	Remarks and references to Appendices
March 2nd/15 BETHUNE	Capt P.A. Lloyd-Jones RAMC } proceeded on Lieut H.H.P. Morton RAMC (CS) } leave ADMS 2 Division visited Officers dressing Station & Main dressing station. No of casualties = 23.	PHG

(73989) W4141—463. 400,000. 9/14. H.&J.Ltd. Forms/C. 2118/10.

Army Form C. 2118.

Instructions regarding War Diaries and Intelligence Summaries are contained in F. S. Regs., Part II. and the Staff Manual respectively. Title pages will be prepared in manuscript.

WAR DIARY
or
~~INTELLIGENCE~~ SUMMARY.
(Erase heading not required.)

Hour, Date, Place	Summary of Events and Information	Remarks and references to Appendices
March 3rd/15 BETHUNE	No of Casualties :- 11	[illegible]

Instructions regarding War Diaries and Intelligence Summaries are contained in F. S. Regs., Part II. and the Staff Manual respectively. Title pages will be prepared in manuscript.

WAR DIARY
or
~~INTELLIGENCE SUMMARY.~~
(Erase heading not required.)

Army Form C. 2118.

Hour, Date, Place	Summary of Events and Information	Remarks and references to Appendices
March 4/15 BETHUNE	Brigadier General the Earl of Cavan returned to duty. No of Casualties = 20 Major P Anderson 1st Kings Lpool Regt Evacuated by M.A.C No 8637. Corpl RANGER H.J RAMC evacuated to Base Hospital	[initials]

(73989) W4141—463. 400,000. 9/14. H.&J.Ltd. Forms/C. 2118/10.

Instructions regarding War Diaries and Intelligence Summaries are contained in F. S. Regs., Part II. and the Staff Manual respectively. Title pages will be prepared in manuscript.

WAR DIARY
or
~~INTELLIGENCE SUMMARY.~~
(Erase heading not required.)

Army Form C. 2118.

Hour, Date, Place	Summary of Events and Information	Remarks and references to Appendices
Mar 5th /15 BETHUNE	Brigadier General H.C. Lowther returned to duty. A.D.M.S. 2 Division visited Officers dressing station and Main dressing station. No of Casualties = 21 2nd Lt N.M. Vibart R.E. 5th Fld Co evacuated by M.A.C. Major H.C. Rochfort-Boyd R.F.A. } also Evacuated Lt F.S. Willis RAMC } by M.A.C.	PAEG

Instructions regarding War Diaries and Intelligence Summaries are contained in F. S. Regs., Part II. and the Staff Manual respectively. Title pages will be prepared in manuscript.

WAR DIARY
or
~~INTELLIGENCE SUMMARY~~.

(*Erase heading not required.*)

Army Form C. 2118.

Hour, Date, Place	Summary of Events and Information	Remarks and references to Appendices
March 6th/15 BETHUNE.	No of Casualties - 17 Lt C. S. O. Fullbrook-Leggatt. D.S.O. 1 R. Berks Capt F. S. Thackeray 2 H.L.I. 2 Lt Scott-Elliott N. 1 Coldstm Captn J. Dare 1st L.N. Lancs (Evacuated by R.A.C.)	RHG

(73989) W4141—463. 400,000. 9/14. H.&J.Ltd. Forms/C. 2118/10.

Instructions regarding War Diaries and Intelligence Summaries are contained in F. S. Regs., Part II. and the Staff Manual respectively. Title pages will be prepared in manuscript.

WAR DIARY
or
~~INTELLIGENCE SUMMARY~~.
(Erase heading not required.)

Army Form C. 2118.

Hour, Date, Place	Summary of Events and Information	Remarks and references to Appendices
March 7th/15 BETHUNE	No of Casualties = 21 Major O.H.L. Nicholson DSO Westyorks Bde major 3rd Brigade evacuated by M.A.C.	[illegible]

(73989) W4141—463. 400,000. 9/14. H.&J.Ltd. Forms/C. 2118/10.

Instructions regarding War Diaries and Intelligence Summaries are contained in F. S. Regs., Part II. and the Staff Manual respectively. Title pages will be prepared in manuscript.

WAR DIARY

or

~~INTELLIGENCE SUMMARY~~.

(Erase heading not required.)

Army Form C. 2118.

Hour, Date, Place	Summary of Events and Information	Remarks and references to Appendices
March 8th/15 BETHUNE	Lieut L. Jones QrMr RAMC returned from leave No of Casualties = 17	PHL

(73989) W4141—463. 400,000. 9/14. H.&J.Ltd. Forms/C. 2118/10.

Army Form C. 2118.

Instructions regarding War Diaries and Intelligence Summaries are contained in F. S. Regs., Part II. and the Staff Manual respectively. Title pages will be prepared in manuscript.

WAR DIARY
or
~~INTELLIGENCE SUMMARY.~~
(Erase heading not required.)

Hour, Date, Place	Summary of Events and Information	Remarks and references to Appendices
March 9th/15 BETHUNE	Captn P. A. Lloyd-Jones RAMC } returned from leave Capt. W. W. Boyce RAMC } Lieut. W McH. McCullagh RAMC }	
	Surgeon General W. G. Macpherson visited dressing station.	PAQ
	No of Casualties :- 16	
	2nd Lt. E R C S Dods Indian Army attd 2nd Munster Fus evacuated by M.A.C.	
	No 5258 Pte Dring RAMC proceeded to ROUEN for duty.	
	No 3226 Pte Tollervey H.R. RAMC evacuated to Base Hospital	

(73989) W4141—463. 400,000. 9/14. H.&J.Ltd. Forms/C. 2118/10.

Instructions regarding War Diaries and Intelligence Summaries are contained in F. S. Regs., Part II. and the Staff Manual respectively. Title pages will be prepared in manuscript.

WAR DIARY
or
~~INTELLIGENCE SUMMARY.~~
(*Erase heading not required.*)

Army Form C. 2118.

Hour, Date, Place	Summary of Events and Information	Remarks and references to Appendices
March 10th/15 BETHUNE.	There was an attack delivered along the line this morning. Wounded started arriving at Dressing station at 10-30 a.m.	
	His Royal Highness The Prince of Wales visited dressing station this afternoon & watched cases being dressed. A.D.M.S. 2nd Division was with him.	
	Following orders published as a routine:–	PHG
	I All cases will be admitted to waiting room on right of main entrance for examination by Orderly Medical Officer who will examine them there. Cases for evacuation will be notified as soon as possible after their arrival.	
	II Lightly wounded cases that do not require dressing will be taken straight to the old Block of buildings to await transport. – This only to apply when casualties are numerous.	

Instructions regarding War Diaries and Intelligence Summaries are contained in F. S. Regs., Part II. and the Staff Manual respectively. Title pages will be prepared in manuscript.

WAR DIARY
or
~~INTELLIGENCE SUMMARY.~~
(*Erase heading not required.*)

Army Form C. 2118.

Hour, Date, Place	Summary of Events and Information	Remarks and references to Appendices
March 10th/15 BETHUNE Contd	III Lightly wounded cases may be dressed and inoculated in the waiting room at the discretion of the Orderly Medical Officer. IV No lying cases requiring dressings will be conveyed to the wards before being dressed, if this can possibly be avoided V Should any lying down cases not require dressing they may be conveyed direct to the wards to await transport. VI Lightly wounded cases will not be on any account taken into the dressing room on the 1st Floor. Lieut W McH McCullagh, 3 NCOs & thirty six Bearers went out and reported to Capt. W.W. Boyce RAMC at 4th (Guards) Infantry Brigade	PAG.

(73989) W4141—463. 400,000. 9/14. H.&J.Ltd. Forms/C. 2118/10.

Instructions regarding War Diaries and Intelligence Summaries are contained in F. S. Regs., Part II. and the Staff Manual respectively. Title pages will be prepared in manuscript.

WAR DIARY
or
~~INTELLIGENCE SUMMARY.~~
(Erase heading not required.)

Army Form C. 2118.

Hour, Date, Place	Summary of Events and Information	Remarks and references to Appendices
March 10th/15 BETHUNE Contd.	at Wood N of canal.	
	They took with them 1 G. S Wagon 1 Scotch cart (Complete with equipment) 1 water Cart.	
	The water Cart fell into a canal owing to the darkness of the night, was dug out again, no traffic being held up	PHG.
	No. of Casualties = 27	
	2 Lt D.B. Curwen 1st L.N. Lancs.	
	2 Lt Cornock-Taylor Lon Scottish.	
	2 Lt A. J. S. Hall. 2 Worcesters	
	2 Lt Campbell. 1 Black Watch	
	Lieut P.C. Scott 1 Kings Lpool	
	2 Lt Richardson 2 S/Staffs	
	Major Romilly D.S.O. Scots Gds.	
	Lt Kingsmill Gren Gds.	
	2nd Lt H Else 1 KRR	
	Lt J S. Townsend 2 S Staffs	
	2 Lt R.P. Ward + R N F.	
	Evacuated by M A C.	

(73989) W4141—463. 400,000. 9/14. H.&J.Ltd. Forms/C. 2118/10.

Instructions regarding War Diaries and Intelligence Summaries are contained in F. S. Regs., Part II. and the Staff Manual respectively. Title pages will be prepared in manuscript.

WAR DIARY
or
~~INTELLIGENCE SUMMARY.~~
(Erase heading not required.)

Army Form C. 2118.

Hour, Date, Place	Summary of Events and Information	Remarks and references to Appendices
March 11th/15 BETHUNE	No of Casualties :- 214	
	Lt. F.C. Blom 1/Irish Gds. } evacuated by M.A.C	PAG
	Lt. A.J. Berry R.E. (T.A.) }	
	Lt. J.W. Garden 1/Black Watch }	
	No 429 Pte. Norman J. Rance. Joined for duty	

(73989) W4141—463. 400,000. 9/14. H.&J.Ltd. Forms/C. 2118/10.

Instructions regarding War Diaries and Intelligence Summaries are contained in F. S. Regs., Part II. and the Staff Manual respectively. Title pages will be prepared in manuscript.

WAR DIARY

or

~~INTELLIGENCE~~ SUMMARY.

(Erase heading not required.)

Army Form C. 2118.

Hour, Date, Place	Summary of Events and Information	Remarks and references to Appendices
March 12/15 BETHUNE	No of Casualties = 50	
	Major R. Crerar London Scottish Lt N. Dowse RAMC att 2/RRR. Lt A H Ludbury 2/Sussex Lt J B Wilmott 2/Worcs Capt E B Greer 1/Irish Gds Lt G. E W. Franklyn R.F.A. Lt S J. Steadman 3rd Somerset } evacuated by 1 M.A.C	PHG
	No 12656 Pte McKeown T. RAMC 17043 " Walker W A do 2571 " Webb J do 3156 " Davies T do 358 " Steele L do 3195 " Martin C. do } Promoted Corporals. 21 3/15, 1 3/15, 1 3/15, 1 3/15, 1 3/15, 1 3/15	

(73989) W4141—463. 400,000. 9/14. H.&J.Ltd. Forms/C. 2118/10.

Army Form C. 2118.

Instructions regarding War Diaries and Intelligence Summaries are contained in F. S. Regs., Part II. and the Staff Manual respectively. Title pages will be prepared in manuscript.

WAR DIARY
or
~~INTELLIGENCE SUMMARY.~~
(*Erase heading not required.*)

Hour, Date, Place	Summary of Events and Information	Remarks and references to Appendices
March 13th/15 BETHUNE	Visited advanced dressing Station under Captn W W Boyce RAMC with the DADMS 2 Division. He has one officer (Lieut W McH McCullagh (SR)) & one Bearer Sub-Division. The advanced dressing Station is situated in a small house which stands back about 30 yards from the road with a garden in front, at a point about 100 yards N of the road at PONT FIXE. There is a house over the road which has been knocked about by shells, where the Motor Ambulance Drivers are accommodated in a cellar	PHS

(73989) W4141—463. 400,000. 9/14. H.&J.Ltd. Forms/C. 2118/10.

Instructions regarding War Diaries and Intelligence Summaries are contained in F. S. Regs., Part II. and the Staff Manual respectively. Title pages will be prepared in manuscript.

WAR DIARY
or
~~INTELLIGENCE SUMMARY.~~
(Erase heading not required.)

Army Form C. 2118.

Hour, Date, Place	Summary of Events and Information	Remarks and references to Appendices
March 13th/15 Contd. BETHUNE	There is one room for patients where about 10 patients could be comfortably put down on left of Hall. On right of Hall there is a room for Medical Officer. Behind these are a kitchen & another room There are stoves in all the rooms The cellars are good. The wounded are brought on wheeled stretchers from the village of GIVENCHY and are collected at all times of the day. GIVENCHY is situated about 800 yards E of	JHG

Instructions regarding War Diaries and Intelligence Summaries are contained in F. S. Regs., Part II. and the Staff Manual respectively. Title pages will be prepared in manuscript.

WAR DIARY
or
~~INTELLIGENCE SUMMARY.~~
(*Erase heading not required.*)

Army Form C. 2118.

Hour, Date, Place	Summary of Events and Information	Remarks and references to Appendices
March 13th/15 Contd BETHUNE	the house. There is an observation station in the Brewery 100 yards to South & the Brewery, particularly the Chimney is constantly shelled. The upper storey of the house is constantly hit by stray bullets. The wounded are evacuated along the road to the south in Motor Ambulances + thence along the La-BASSE Rd through BEUVRY to BETHUNE The German trenches can be plainly seen about a distance of 1100 yards away. No of Casualties :- 39. Lt G R H Rouquette No 7 M Batty Evacuated by MAC	PHG

(73989) W4141—463. 400,000. 9/14. H.&J.Ltd. Forms/C. 2118/10.

Instructions regarding War Diaries and Intelligence Summaries are contained in F. S. Regs., Part II. and the Staff Manual respectively. Title pages will be prepared in manuscript.

WAR DIARY
or
~~INTELLIGENCE SUMMARY.~~
(Erase heading not required.)

Army Form C. 2118.

Hour, Date, Place	Summary of Events and Information	Remarks and references to Appendices
March 14/15 BETHUNE	No 7 Motor Ambulance Convoy is clearing all the Field Ambulances No of Casualties :- 22 2/Lt H.D. Sprunt 2 S/Staffs 2/Lt Gunstone 1/Irish Gds Lt H.R. Moore 3/London Regt Lt E.K. Stevenson 1/Cold Gds } evacuated by M.A.C No 18459 Pte Daniels V. Rance evacuated to Base Hospital	[illegible initials]

(73989) W4141—463. 400,000. 9/14. H.&J.Ltd. Forms/C. 2118/10.

Instructions regarding War Diaries and Intelligence Summaries are contained in F. S. Regs., Part II. and the Staff Manual respectively. Title pages will be prepared in manuscript.

WAR DIARY
or
~~INTELLIGENCE SUMMARY.~~
(Erase heading not required.)

Army Form C. 2118.

Hour, Date, Place	Summary of Events and Information	Remarks and references to Appendices
March 15/15 BETHUNE	Commanding Officer visited with the D A D M S 2 Division the advanced Dressing station. Shell went into house and burst ~~on back wall~~ in the kitchen. No Casualties. Another shell burst close by. Personnel shifted into cellars No of Casualties = 41 Lt R. A. G. Whistler 2 HLI } Lt Johnstone 4/RWF } Capt B. L. Mariner RFA } Capt D. R. Inskip 59 Rifles } evacuated by MAC	[initials]

(73989) W4141—463. 400,000. 9/14. H.&J.Ltd. Forms/C. 2118/10.

Instructions regarding War Diaries and Intelligence Summaries are contained in F. S. Regs., Part II. and the Staff Manual respectively. Title pages will be prepared in manuscript.

WAR DIARY
or
~~INTELLIGENCE SUMMARY.~~
(Erase heading not required.)

Army Form C. 2118.

Hour, Date, Place	Summary of Events and Information	Remarks and references to Appendices
March 16/15 BETHUNE	No of Casualties :- 39	
	Bri General F.C. Carter 24 Inf Bde 8th Div evacuated by M.A.C	
	2 Lt J. Smith R.F.A. } evacuated by M.A.C.	
	Lt P. Wright R.F.A. }	
	Capt J A Knight 1/H.L.I. }	
	Capt A D Mitchell 4/Suffolks }	PHG

(73989) W4141—463. 400,000. 9/14. H.&J.Ltd. Forms/C. 2118/10.

Army Form C. 2118.

Instructions regarding War Diaries and Intelligence Summaries are contained in F. S. Regs., Part II. and the Staff Manual respectively. Title pages will be prepared in manuscript.

WAR DIARY

or

~~INTELLIGENCE SUMMARY.~~

(Erase heading not required.)

Hour, Date, Place	Summary of Events and Information	Remarks and references to Appendices
March 17/15 BETHUNE	No of Casualties = 31. Lt Edgecombe 9/HLI evacuated by M.A.C.	PHG

(73989) W4141—463. 400,000. 9/14. H.&J.Ltd. Forms/C. 2118/10.

Instructions regarding War Diaries and Intelligence Summaries are contained in F. S. Regs., Part II. and the Staff Manual respectively. Title pages will be prepared in manuscript.

WAR DIARY
or
INTELLIGENCE SUMMARY.
(Erase heading not required.)

Army Form C. 2118.

Hour, Date, Place	Summary of Events and Information	Remarks and references to Appendices
March 18/15	No of Casualties = 37	
BETHUNE	Lt D. E. Trafford 2/Cold Gds. evacuated by M.A.C	
	No 2679. Pte Randall. S. RAMC proceeded to 2 Divl Ammn Column for duty	[illegible initials]
	No 5680 Pte Simeoker RAMC arrived for duty	

(73989) W4141—463. 400,000. 9/14. H.&J.Ltd. Forms/C. 2118/10.

Army Form C. 2118.

Instructions regarding War Diaries and Intelligence Summaries are contained in F. S. Regs., Part II. and the Staff Manual respectively. Title pages will be prepared in manuscript.

WAR DIARY

or

~~INTELLIGENCE SUMMARY.~~

(*Erase heading not required.*)

Hour, Date, Place	Summary of Events and Information	Remarks and references to Appendices
March 19/15 BETHUNE	No of Casualties = 19. Capt E A Trafford 11th Middlesex att. 59 Rifles	PHG

(73989) W4141—463. 400,000. 9/14. H.&J.Ltd. Forms/C. 2118/10.

Instructions regarding War Diaries and Intelligence Summaries are contained in F. S. Regs., Part II. and the Staff Manual respectively. Title pages will be prepared in manuscript.

WAR DIARY
or
~~INTELLIGENCE SUMMARY.~~
(Erase heading not required.)

Army Form C. 2118.

Hour, Date, Place	Summary of Events and Information	Remarks and references to Appendices
March 20/15 BETHUNE	D.M.S 1st Army accompanied by his Staff Officer & A.D.M.S. 2 Division brought the Director General of the French Medical Services to the Dressing Station in the Afternoon–	
	The Director General made a speech to the Armonier the sisters, in which he thanked them for their amiability in facilitating the work of the English Medical Service BETHUNE.	[initials]
	No of Casualties = 26	
	Lt. A. N. V. Moore 1st Manchesters evacuated by M.A.C.	
	No 3761 Pte Cooper J. R.A.M.C. evacuated to Base Hospital	

(73989) W4141—463. 400,000. 9/14. H.&J.Ltd. Forms/C. 2118/10.

Instructions regarding War Diaries and Intelligence Summaries are contained in F. S. Regs., Part II. and the Staff Manual respectively. Title pages will be prepared in manuscript.

WAR DIARY
or
~~INTELLIGENCE SUMMARY.~~
(Erase heading not required.)

Army Form C. 2118.

Hour, Date, Place	Summary of Events and Information	Remarks and references to Appendices
March 21/15 BETHUNE	The Director General of Medical Services (Sir A T. Slogett. and Head Quarter Staff visited the officers' Dressing Station.	[initials]
	No of Casualties = 25	
	2nd Lt G.W. Stibbings 4/Suffolks Lt J H Steward 2/M F. Major H.J. Ramsay 1st Div Artillery Capt E.N. Buchan 1/Manchesters Lt J.S. Rich 1/Kings Lt W.H.J. Carpendale 1st Gurkha Rifles Lt J.T. Shute 3 Norwich Capt J.S. Egerton 2 Cold Gds } Evacuated by M.A.C.	

Instructions regarding War Diaries and Intelligence Summaries are contained in F. S. Regs., Part II. and the Staff Manual respectively. Title pages will be prepared in manuscript.

WAR DIARY
or
~~INTELLIGENCE SUMMARY.~~
(Erase heading not required.)

Army Form C. 2118.

Hour, Date, Place	Summary of Events and Information	Remarks and references to Appendices
March 22/15 BETHUNE	Capt. T.S. Blackwell R.A.M.C. proceeded on leave	
	No of Casualties = 34	
	Lt. P.P. Curtis 15/Hussars Capt E.B. Gregge-Hopwood 2 Cold Gds Lt. R.M. Purvis 1 Black Watch Lt. J.A.M. Scobie 59th Scinde Rifles Lt. Fitzmaurice R.E. 21st Coy } evacuated by M.A.C.	DHG
	No 36845 Pte Fazackley W.E. 34661 " Hughes G. 47820 " Lumley T. 33457 " Luckett J.A. 47721 " Hawick R } arrived for duty from No 4 Stationary Hospital	

Instructions regarding War Diaries and Intelligence Summaries are contained in F. S. Regs., Part II. and the Staff Manual respectively. Title pages will be prepared in manuscript.

WAR DIARY
or
~~INTELLIGENCE SUMMARY.~~

(*Erase heading not required.*)

Army Form C. 2118.

Hour, Date, Place	Summary of Events and Information	Remarks and references to Appendices
March 23/15 BETHUNE.	Col: Sir Antony Bowlby and Col: Sir W. P. Herringham visited Dressing Station & held Consultation regarding Lieut Mackenzie R.A.M.C. attached 1. H.L.I.	PHG
	No of casualties :- 21	
	Major J.H. Lang-Sims 4th Kings } Lt N. Draycott-Wood 2 S/Staffs } evacuated by M.A.C	

(73989) W4141—463. 400,000. 9/14. H.&J.Ltd. Forms/C. 2118/10.

Instructions regarding War Diaries and Intelligence Summaries are contained in F. S. Regs., Part II. and the Staff Manual respectively. Title pages will be prepared in manuscript.

WAR DIARY

or

~~INTELLIGENCE SUMMARY.~~

(Erase heading not required.)

Army Form C. 2118.

Hour, Date, Place	Summary of Events and Information	Remarks and references to Appendices
March 24th/15	No of Casualties = 30.	
BETHUNE	Lt T.W.P. Evans 2 S Staffs } evacuated by M.A.C. Lt W.K. MacDonald 5th Kings }	PAHG

(73989) W4141—463. 400,000. 9/14. H.&J.Ltd. Forms/C. 2118/10.

Army Form C. 2118.

Instructions regarding War Diaries and Intelligence Summaries are contained in F. S. Regs., Part II. and the Staff Manual respectively. Title pages will be prepared in manuscript.

WAR DIARY
or
~~INTELLIGENCE SUMMARY~~.
(*Erase heading not required.*)

Hour, Date, Place	Summary of Events and Information		Remarks and references to Appendices
March 25th/15	No of Casualties = 14		
BETHUNE.	Lt W. H. Ockleston 5/Kings	evacuated by M. A. C.	PRG
	Lt J. E. G. Nugent. 1/Irish Gds		
	2/Lt G. R. G. Smyth 7/Kings		
	2/Lt T. Fawdry 1/L. Lancs		
	Lt C. Ellis 5/Kings		

Instructions regarding War Diaries and Intelligence Summaries are contained in F. S. Regs., Part II. and the Staff Manual respectively. Title pages will be prepared in manuscript.

WAR DIARY
or
~~INTELLIGENCE~~ SUMMARY.
(Erase heading not required.)

Army Form C. 2118.

Hour, Date, Place	Summary of Events and Information	Remarks and references to Appendices
March 26/15 BETHUNE	The Chief Matron visited the Dressing Station to-day. No of Casualties = 20. Lt H. H. Jackson 15th Hussars Capt E. Gore-Brown 8th City of London Lt Mackenzie RAMC attd 1 HLI 2nd Lieut C. R. Horley 2 Oxfords 2nd Lieut R. E. Rose R.E. 26 Coy 2nd Lieut N. V. Trubshawe 1 Kings } Evacuated by MAC	[initials]

(73989) W4141—463. 400,000. 9/14. H.&J.Ltd. Forms/C. 2118/10.

Army Form C. 2118.

Instructions regarding War Diaries and Intelligence Summaries are contained in F. S. Regs., Part II. and the Staff Manual respectively. Title pages will be prepared in manuscript.

WAR DIARY
or
~~INTELLIGENCE SUMMARY.~~
(Erase heading not required.)

Hour, Date, Place	Summary of Events and Information	Remarks and references to Appendices
March 27/15. BETHUNE.	N° of Casualties - 14. Lieut. B.N. Murphy. R.A.M.C. returned from leave	RAHG

(73989) W4141—463. 400,000. 9/14. H.&J.Ltd. Forms/C. 2118/10.

Instructions regarding War Diaries and Intelligence Summaries are contained in F. S. Regs., Part II. and the Staff Manual respectively. Title pages will be prepared in manuscript.

WAR DIARY
or
~~INTELLIGENCE~~ SUMMARY.
(Erase heading not required.)

Army Form C. 2118.

Hour, Date, Place	Summary of Events and Information	Remarks and references to Appendices
March 28/15 BETHUNE	Brigade Major V. Vivian. 4th (Guards) Infantry Brigade 2nd Lt W. T. F. LATHAM. 1st Connaughts 4th London Lt A. B. Lucy evacuated by M. A. C.	
	No of Casualties = 15.	
	No 9239 Pte McDiarmid T. R.A.M.C. arrived for duty from No 24 Field Ambulance.	
	G.O.C. 4th Infantry Brigade visited Dressing Station	
	Lieut. T. Bourne - Price R.A.M.C. returned from leave	PHQ

Army Form C. 2118.

Instructions regarding War Diaries and Intelligence Summaries are contained in F. S. Regs., Part II. and the Staff Manual respectively. Title pages will be prepared in manuscript.

WAR DIARY
or
INTELLIGENCE SUMMARY.

(Erase heading not required.)

Hour, Date, Place	Summary of Events and Information	Remarks and references to Appendices
March 29th/15	No of Casualties = 28	
BETHUNE	Capt A.P. Strange 1/Berks } evacuated by	
	Lieut D.C. Parsons 1/Irish Gds } M.A.C.	
	No 7978 Pte W. Bruce RAMC } arrived for duty	
	8168 " C Ballard do } from No 4 Statn H.	
	Sur General T J O'Donnell DSO & Lt Col	
	P. Evans visited the dressing station.	[initials]

(73989) W4141—463. 400,000. 9/14. H.&J.Ltd. Forms/C. 2118/10.

Instructions regarding War Diaries and Intelligence Summaries are contained in F. S. Regs., Part II. and the Staff Manual respectively. Title pages will be prepared in manuscript.

WAR DIARY
or
~~INTELLIGENCE SUMMARY.~~
(Erase heading not required.)

Army Form C. 2118.

Hour, Date, Place	Summary of Events and Information	Remarks and references to Appendices
March 30/15	No of Casualties = 36	
BETHUNE	Capt. Lord de Freyne 1st S.W.B. } admitted to Lieut. Sir R. J. M. Walker 2 Colds Gds } Dressing Station	
	6 Motor Ambulance Wagons arrived and ~~taken~~ on strength = 5 Sunbeams and 1 Ford	
	052752 Corpl Rylands F 052774 Pte. Walsh J. 052762 " Pierson A.S. 050419 " Turvey G.H. 050549 " Gladwin E. 37057 " Dibble F.W. 050836 " Hoyle A.E. 049160 " Horne F.E. 052767 " Stubbefield A. 052797 " A King 050849 " Levy H 052751 " Rule R. } A.S.C. Motor Ambulance Drivers arrived for duty	PMG

Army Form C. 2118.

Instructions regarding War Diaries and Intelligence Summaries are contained in F. S. Regs., Part II. and the Staff Manual respectively. Title pages will be prepared in manuscript.

WAR DIARY
or
~~INTELLIGENCE SUMMARY.~~
(Erase heading not required.)

Hour, Date, Place	Summary of Events and Information		Remarks and references to Appendices
March 30/15	Lieut G. F. Gregory 1st R Berks	Evacuated by M. A. C.	PHG
Contd.	2/Lieut. B. M. Gee 17th Batty R.F.A.		
BETHUNE.	Lieut E. P. Orr-Ewing 1st Scots Gds.		
	2/Lieut. F. C. Davis 3rd London Regt.		
	Captn R. Williams R.E. (Royl. Anglesey)		
	Captn T. O. Bury 4th R.W.F.		

(73989) W4141—463. 400,000. 9/14. H.&J.Ltd. Forms/C. 2118/10.

No 4 Field Ambulance

Evacuation returns 8 am. 5-15.

Officers Nil

O. Ranks. Sitting 2
Lying Nil

OC No 7 MAC [illegible] for OC No 4 F Amb.
Lieut. RAMC

[illegible]

[illegible]

No 4 Field Ambulance

Evacuation Return 3pm 1/3/15

Officers 2*

Other Ranks Lying 6
Sitting 9

*1 Officer at Officer's Dressing Station +
1 Officer at Main Dressing Station

OC No 4 Motor Convoy

[signature]

Lieut RAMC
for OC No 4 Field Ambl

[initials]

No 4 Field Ambulance.

Evacuation Return 3pm 2/3/15

Lying 3 *
Sitting 12

* This includes 1 case suspected Enteric for transfer to Lillers.

O.C. No 7 Motor Ambulance } J J O'Keeffe
Capt RAMC
for O.C. No 4 Fd Amb.

[illegible]

No 4 Field Ambulance

Evacuation Return

Officer Commanding
[illegible]

AA MAC

[illegible] 2 - 15

[illegible]
for OC No 4 Fld Amb.

4   5 *

[illegible]   4

* Includes 1 case [illegible] for transfer to [illegible] LERS

O.C. No. [illegible] [illegible]

[illegible] R. [illegible]
for O.C. No. 4 [illegible] Amb.

No 4 Field Ambulance

Evacuation Return 3pm. 3-3-15

MKH.

Lying. 4
Sitting. ~~3~~ 4 *

Includes 1 case for transfer to No 4 Clearing H. LILLERS

OC No 7 Motor Convoy

J S Dunn [illegible]
Capt R A M C
for OC No 4 Field Ambl.

Evact Return
5-3-15

Officers :- 1 Lying
O Ranks 4 Lying

PMG

O.C. No 7 M.A.C.
5-3-15

~~Capt~~ Lieut Raab
OC No 4 Field Ambce

Instructions regarding War Diaries and Intelligence Summaries are contained in F. S. Regs., Part II. and the Staff Manual respectively. Title pages will be prepared in manuscript.

WAR DIARY

or

~~INTELLIGENCE SUMMARY.~~

(Erase heading not required.)

Army Form C. 2118.

Hour, Date, Place	Summary of Events and Information	Remarks and references to Appendices
March 31/15 BETHUNE	No of Casualties :- 30 Capt. T. S. Blackwell R.A.M.C. returned from leave	

(73989) W4141—463. 400,000. 9/14. H.&J.Ltd. Forms/C. 2118/10.

No 4 Field Ambulance

Evacuation Return 3pm

Officers 2
Other Ranks Lying 3
Sitting 5

5-3-15

J J O'Kieffe
Capt RAMC
for OC No 4 Fd Amb

No 4 Field Ambulance

Evacuation Return 3 pm

Officers 4

Other Ranks Lying 13 *
Sitting 1.

* The total includes 1 case suspected enteric for transfer to LILLERS.

[illegible signature]

Lieut. RAMC.
for OC No 4 Field Ambulance

OC No 7 Motor Convoy
6-3-15

54
15/20

56
20/76
20/56

53

No 4 Field Ambulance

Evacuation return 3 pm

Officers 1

Other Ranks Lying 2
Sitting 4

OC No 4 Motor Convoy
4 · 3 - 15

J B Sept.
Lieut RAMC
for OC No 4 Field Amb

No 4 Field Ambulance

Evacuation Return 3pm

Lying 4
Sitting 8

O.C. No 7 Motor Convoy
8.3.15

[illegible]
Lieut RAMC
for O.C. No 4 Field Ambl.

No 4 Field Ambulance

Evacuation return 3 pm

Officers 1 *

Other Ranks Lying: 8
Sitting: 6

* This officer is for evacuation from the Main Dressing Station

9·3·15

J J O'Keeffe
Capt RAMC
for OC No 4 Field Ambl.

No 7 MAC Section
Evacuation Return

Officers	Lying	4
Men	Lying	12
Men	Sitting	12

PAY.

Please send wagons for these at once

Time 1 pm } 10 3. 15

P.A. Lloyd Jones
Capt RAMC
O.C. 4 I amb

O.C. [illegible] Motor Convoy

Evacuation Return

Officers	Lying 2	
Men	Lying 8	
Men	Sitting 12	

PAH

Please send wagons for these at once

P A [illegible]

Capt. R.A.M.C.

O.C. No 4 Field Amb.

Time 2.15 pm.

10 - 3 - 15

O.C.
No. 7 Motor Convoy

Evacuation return.

Officers	Lying	2
Men	Lying	12
	Sitting.	8.

PAL

Please send wagons for these at once.

P. A. Lloyd Jones
Capt R.A.M.C.
O.C. 1/2nd Field Amb.

Time 4-40
10 · 3 · 15

OC

No 4 Motor Convoy.

Please send 5 Motor Ambulances.

at once

P.A. Lloyd Jones
Capt RAMC
OC No 22 Field Ambl.

PKG.

6-30 pm
10-3-15

OC
1 No 4 Motor Convoy.

Evacuation Return.

Lying 24

Sitting 10.

PAL

Please send wagons for these at once.

P. A. Lloyd Jones.
Capt RAMC
OC No 4 Field Ambl.

Time
11-3-15

OC

No 7 Motor Convoy.

Evacuation Return.

Officers 2

Men Lying 4

Sitting 10

PHG

P. A. Lloyd Jones.

Capt RAMC

OC No 4 Field Amb

Time
11-3-15

No. 4 Field Ambulance

Evacuation Return.

Lying 7

Sitting 8

O.C.
No. 4 Motor Convoy
Time 3 pm 11-3-15

P. A. Lloyd Jones.

Capt R.A.M.C.
O.C. No. 4 Field Amb.

O.C. [illegible] Motor Convoy

Evacuation Return.

Lying 3

Sitting 3

Please send wagons for these.

P.A. Lloyd Jones.

Capt. R.A.M.C.
O.C. No 4 Field Amb.

Time 11-30 am
12 · 3 · 15

No 4 Field Ambulance

Evacuation Return.

Officers 2

Other Ranks Lying 1
Sitting 2

Please send wagons for these at 4 pm.

O.C. No 7 Motor Convoy
Time 3-10pm
12 3 - 15

R.A. Lloyd Jones
Capt R.A.M.C.
O.C. No 4 Fd Amb

No 4 Field Ambulance

Evacuation Return

Officers 3 *
Other Ranks 1.

This total includes 2 cases of suspected Enteric for Transfer to LILLERS.

Please send cars for these.

P. A. Lloyd Jones

Capt. R.A.M.C.
O.C. No 4 Field Amb.

O.C. No 7 Motor Convoy.
6 pm 12-3-15

[illegible] Field Ambulance

Evacuation Return

Officers Lying 1 (From [illegible] Dressing Station.)

Other Ranks Lying 6

Please send wagons for these at 2 pm.

P. A. Lloyd Jones
Capt. R.A.M.C.
for O.C. [illegible] Field Amb.

O.C.
[illegible] Motor Convoy

13 - 3 - 15 12-10 pm

No 4 Field Ambulance

Numbers requiring to be evacuated to L of C.

		Sick	Wounded
Officers	Lying	–	–
	Sitting	–	–
Other Ranks	Lying	2	–
	Sitting	4	–

A D M S
2nd Div
5pm 13 · 3 · 15

J S Blumson [?]
Capt R A M C
O C No 4 Field Ambl.

PHG [?]

No. 4 Field Ambulance.

Evacuation Return, 8 am. 14/3/15.

Lying - 5.
Sitting - 5.

[signature]

Capt. RAMC.
for OC. No. 4 Field Ambce

[initials]

OC. No. 7. MAC.

No. 4 Field Ambulance.

Numbers requiring to be evacuated to L of C.

		Sick	Wndd.
Officers	Lying	–	–
	Sitting	–	–
Other Rks.	Lying	4	1
	Sitting	4	1

ADMS. 2nd Divn
9am. 14/3/15.

P. A. Lloyd Jones
Capt. RAMC.
OC. No. 4 Field Ambce

No 4 Field Ambulance

Evacuation Return

Officers 1

Other Ranks. Lying. 6

Sitting. 10.

O.C. No 4 Motor Convoy

14 – 3 – 15

P.A. Lloyd Jones

Capt R.A.M.C.

O.C. No 4 Fd Ambl.

No 4 Field Ambulance

Numbers requiring to be evacuated to L of C

		Sick.	Wounded.
Officers	Lying	—	—
	Sitting	—	—
O Ranks	Lying	—	—
	Sitting	—	—

A D M S
2nd Div
5pm 14·3·15

J S Dunn[illegible]
Capt RAMC
for OC No 4 Field Ambl.
(on duty)

[illegible]

No 4 Field Ambulance

Evacuation Return, 15/3/15 8 a.m.

Lying - 3.
Sitting - 5.

[signature]

Lieut. RAMC
for OC. No. 4 Field Ambce

[initials]

~~At~~ OC. No. 7 M. A.C.
15/3/15 8 a.m.

5

5 L

4 S

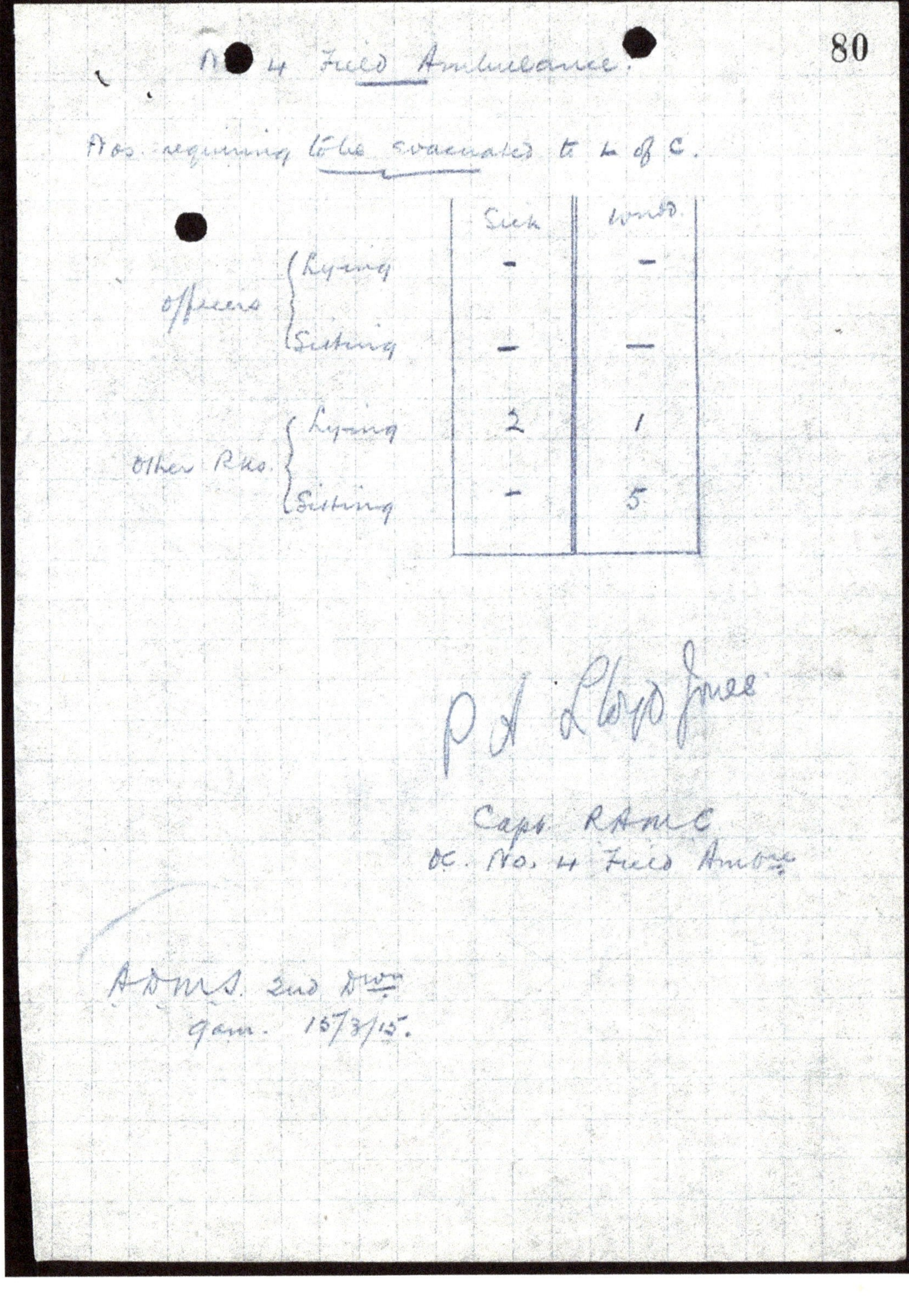
80

No 4 Field Ambulance.

Nos. requiring to be evacuated to L of C.

		Sick	Wdd.
Officers	Lying	–	–
	Sitting	–	–
Other Rks.	Lying	2	1
	Sitting	–	5

P A Lloyd Jones

Capt. RAMC
OC. No. 4 Field Ambce.

ADMS. 2nd Divn.
9am. 15/3/15.

No 2 Field Ambulance.

Evacuation Return.

Officers 5

Other Ranks Lying. 6

Sitting. 8

O.C. No 4 Motor Convoy
Time
15 3 15

P. K. Lloyd Jones
Capt R.A.M.C.
O.C. No 2 Fd Amb.

No. 2 Field Ambulance

Nos requiring to be evacuated to L of C.

		Sick	Wounded
Officers	Lying	—	—
	Sitting	—	—
Other Ranks	Lying	—	—
	Sitting	—	—

A D M S
2nd Div
15/3/15

J. S. [illegible]
Capt RAMC
for OC No 2 Fd Ambl.
on duty

[illegible]

No. 4 Field Ambulance.

Evacuation Return. 8am 16/3/15.

Lying 2
Sitting 1

Officers 1.

[signature]

Lieut RAMC.
for O.C. No. 4 Fd. Ambce

[initials]

OC No. 7 MAC.
16/3/15 8am.

No 4 Field Ambulance

Nos requiring to be evacuated to L of C.

		Sick	Wndd
Officers	Lying	1	—
	Sitting	—	—
Other Rks	Lying	—	2
	Sitting	—	1

P A Lloyd Jones

Capt RAMC.
OC No 4 Fd. Ambce

ADMS. 2nd Divn
16/3/15 9am

No 4 Field Ambulance

Evacuation Return

Officers 4

Other Ranks Lying 5

Sitting 6

O.C. No 7 Motor Convoy }
3 pm 16/3/15 }

J. J. O'Keeffe
Capt RAMC
for O.C. No 4 Fd Amb.

[illegible]

Cav Field Ambulance

Nos requiring to be evacuated to L of C.

		Sick	Wounded
Officers	Lying	—	—
	Sitting	—	—
O Ranks	Lying	—	—
	Sitting	—	—

A.D.M.S. }
2nd Div }
16/3/15 }

J J O'Keeffe
Capt RAMC
for OC Cav Fd Ambl
on duty

DRY

No 4 Field Ambulance RETURNS 2

Evacuation Return, 17/3/15 - 8 am.

Lying - 2.
Sitting - 4.

Officers. Nil.

[illegible signature]

Lieut RAMC.
for OC No. 4 Fd. Ambce

[illegible initials]

OC. No 7 M.A.C.

No 4 Field Ambulance

Evacuation Return 17·3·15

Lying 7
Sitting 8

R/C No 7 Motor Convoy
3pm. 17·3·15

J. J. O'Keeffe
Capt RAMC
for O.C. No 4 Fd Amb.

[illegible]

10

No. 4 Field Ambulance

Evacuation Return, 8 a.m. 18/3/15.

Lying – 2
Sitting – 4.

Officers 1

[signature]

Capt. R.A.M.C.
for O.C. No. 4 Field Ambce

[initials]

O.C. No. 7. M.A.C.

No 4 Field Ambulance

Evacuation Return 3pm.

Sitting. 7

O.C. No 1 Motor Convoy.
18 3 - 15

Basil Humphry
Lt. R.A.M.C.
for ~~Capt~~ R.A.M.C.
O.C. No 4 Field Amb.

DML

No 4 Field Ambulance

Evacuation Return.

Officers 1

Other Ranks Lying 3

Sitting 7

P. A. Lloyd Jones.

OC No 7 Motor Convoy
3pm 19 . 3 . 15

Capt R A M C
OC No 4 Field Ambulance

No. 4 Field Ambulance

Evacuation Return 8 a.m. 20/3/15.

Lying 2.
Sitting 7.

Officer 1.

[illegible]

Lieut. RAMC.
for OC. No. 4 Fd. Ambce

[illegible]

OC No. 7 MAC.

No 4 Field Ambulance

Evacuation Return.

Officers 3 (3)

Other Ranks Lying 2

Sitting 4

O.C. No 4 Motor Convoy
3pm 20.3.15

J J O'Keeffe
Capt R.A.M.C.
for O.C. No 4 Field Ambl.

JRH

No 4 Field Ambulance.

Evacuation Return, 8 am. 21/3/15.

Lying - Nil
Sitting - Nil

Officers - 2.

[signature]
Capt. RAMC.
for OC. No 4 Fd. Ambce.

OC. No 7. M.AC.

No 4 Field Ambulance

Evacuation Return.

Officers 1

other Ranks: Lying 8

Sitting 5

O.C. No 7 Motor Convoy

3pm 21-3-15

J S Manson

Capt RAMC

for. O.C. No 4 Field Ambl.

PRH

No 4 Field Ambulance

Evacuation Return 3pm.

Officers 2 Lying
1 Sitting

Other Ranks Lying 7 *
Sitting. 8

* 1 Case Suspected Diphtheria for transfer to No 4 Casualty Clearing LILLERS

OC/ No 4 Motor Convoy

J B Scott Lieut
RMO
Capt [illegible]
for OC No 4 Fd Amb

[illegible]

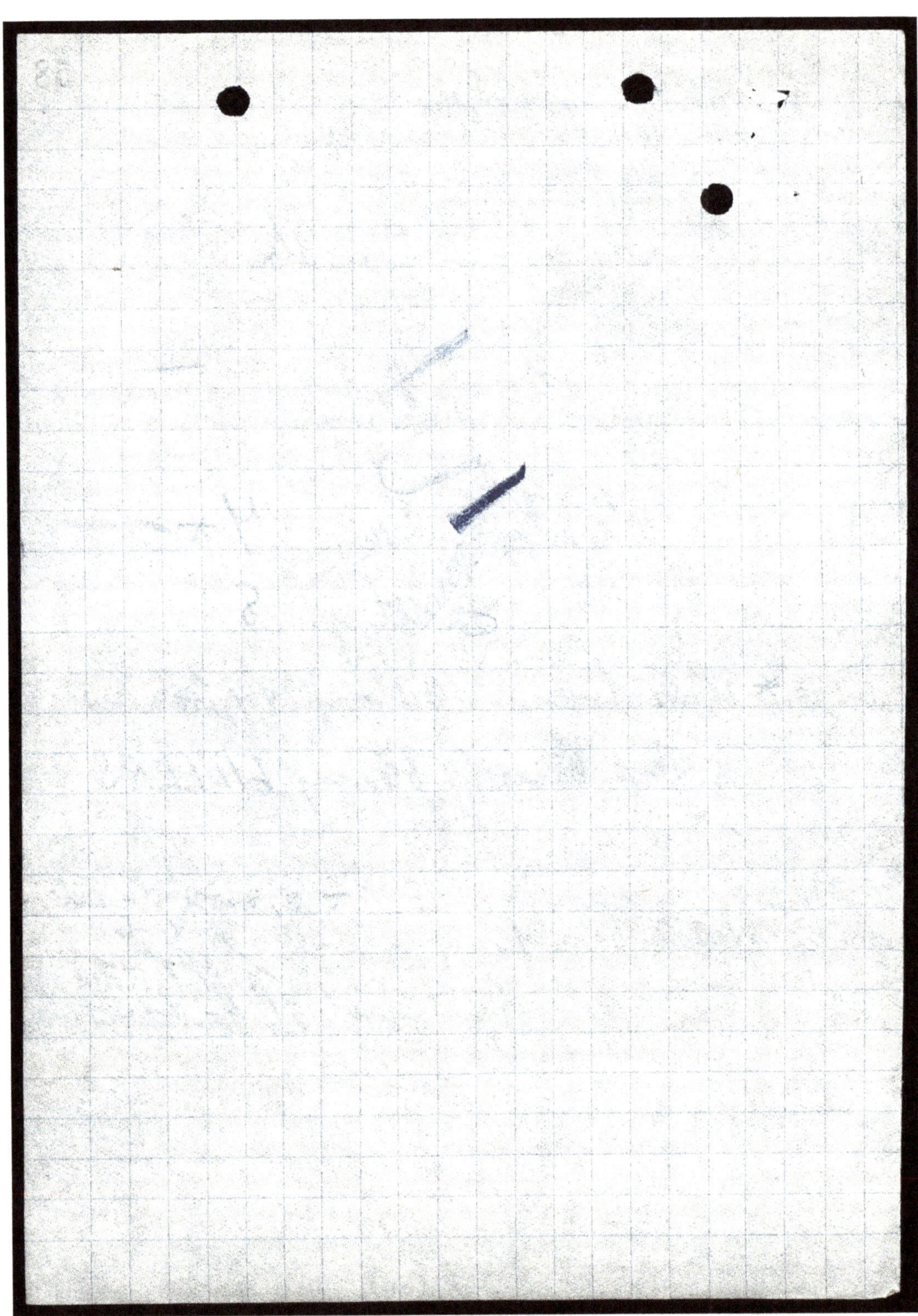

No. 4 Field Ambulance

Evacuation Return. 8am. 23/2/15.

Lying 2.
Sitting 5.

J B Scott
Lieut. RAMC.
for OC. No. 4 Fd. Amb.

23/2/15.

[illegible]

No 4 Field Ambulance

Evacuation Return 3pm

Officers 2

Other Ranks: Lying 4

Sitting 10.

O.C. No 4 Motor Convoy
23. 3. 15

[illegible]
for Lieut
Capt RAMC
O.C. No 4 Field Ambl.

No. 4 Field Ambulance

Evacuation Return. 24/3/15. 8 am.

Lying – Nil.
Sitting – 5.

Officers – 2.

[illegible]

Lieut. RAMC
for O.C. No 4 Fd. Ambce

[illegible]

OC No. 7 MAC

No 4 Field Ambulance

Evacuation Return. 3pm

Lying 3

Sitting 4

OC No 4 Motor Convoy.
24 - 3 - 15

[signature]
for Capt RAMC
OC No 4 Field Ambl.

[initials]

84

No. 4 Field Ambulance.

Evacuation Return, 8am. 25/3/15.

Lying - 1.
Sitting - None

Officers - 2.

[signature]

Capt RAMC.
for OC. No. 4 Fd. Ambce.

O.C. No 7 M.A.C.

[initials]

No 4 Field Ambulance

Evacuation Return 3pm

Officers 4

Other Ranks Lying 3

Sitting 6

OC No 4 Motor Convoy
25 - 3 - 15

for J B Scott Lieut
Capt RAMC
OC No 4 Field Am

PRL

No. 4 Field Ambulance

Evacuation Return – 8am 26/3/15.

Lying . Nil
Sitting . Nil.

Officers 2.

J B Scott.
Lieut. RAMC.
for O.C. No 4 Field Amb^ce

O.C. No 7. M.A.C.

[illegible]

No 4 Field Ambulance.

Evacuation Return 3pm

Officers 4 *.

Other Ranks Lying ~~[illegible]~~ 5 [illegible]

Sitting ~~4~~ 4 [illegible]

2 Officers for evacuation from Main Dressing Station

OC/No 7 M.A.C.
26-3-15

P. A. Lloyd Jones
Capt R.A.M.C.
OC No 4 Field Ambulance

18

No. 4 Field Ambulance

Evacuation Returns. 8 am 28/3/15.

Lying 1.
Sitting 2.

[signature]

Capt. RAMC.
for OC No. 4 Field Amb^ce

[initials]

O.C. No. 7. M.A.C.

No 4 Field Ambulance

Evacuation Return 3pm 28/3/18

Officers 3

Other Ranks. Lying 3
Sitting 4.

A. H. Lovell Lt. RAMC
for
Capt. RAMC.
OC. No 4 F. S amb.

O.C. Motor Am. Convoy
No 7.

No 4 Field Ambulance

Evacuation Return – 8 am 29/3/15.

Lying 2.

Sitting 2

Basil T Murphy

Lieut RAMC

for OC No 4 Fd. Amb.

[illegible]

OC No 7. MAC

No 4 Field Ambulance
Evacuation Return 3 pm

Officers . 3 .

Other Ranks Lying . — 1

Sitting . — 2

O.C. No 4 Motor Convoy
29 - 3 - 15

P. A. Lloyd Jones

Capt. R.A.M.C.
O.C. No 4 Field Ambulance

No 4 Field Ambulance

Evacuation return 3pm

Officers 6 *

Other Ranks Lying 8

Sitting 5

* One officer (Lying) to be evacuated from Main D. S.

O.C. No 7 Motor Convoy
30 3 15

P. A. Lloyd Jones
Capt RAMC
O.C. No 4 Field Amb

No 4 Field Ambulance

Evacuation Return 3pm.

Lying. 6.

Sitting. ~~5~~ 10

O.C. No 4 Motor Convoy
31-3-15

Basil N Murphy
Lt. R.A.M.C.
~~Capt R.A.M.C~~
for O.C. No 4 Field Ambulance

PMG

No 4 Field Ambulance

Table showing No of sick & wounded [illegible] during 24 hours ended [illegible] 1/3/15

Unit	[illegible]	[illegible]	[illegible]	[illegible]
Gren. Gds	–	–	[illegible]	4
2 Coldm	–	–	1	–
3 Cold	–	–	1	–
1 Irish	1	–	[illegible]	–
1 Herts (T)	–	–	1	1
1 Berks	1	–	–	–
[illegible] HLI	–	–	–	–
2 S Staffs	1	–	–	–
R.E. [illegible]	–	–	–	–
[illegible]	–	–	–	1
KRR	–	–	–	1
R [illegible]	–	–	–	–
[illegible]	–	–	–	–
RFA 4 [illegible]	–	–	–	–
TOTAL	3	–	8	8

[illegible]

Lieut. [illegible] SMITE [illegible] Berks [illegible]

Lieut. [illegible] INNES 1 [illegible] [illegible]

" A SILCOCK 2. S.R. Staffs.

J S [illegible]

[illegible] 2 Div.

1-3-15

Capt. RAMC

for OC No 4 Field Amb.

No 4 Field Ambulance
Table shewing No of Sick & Wounded by Units adm'd during 24 hours ended 9 am 2 March /15

2 Division	Officers Sick	Officers Wnd	O Ranks Sick	O Ranks Wnd
2 Cold Gds			3	–
3 " "			3	–
2 Gren "			1	–
1 Irish "			1	–
1 Berks			–	1
1 Kings			1	2
2 Wores			–	1
2 S. Staffs			1	–
1 Herts			1	1
2 HLI			–	1
34th Bde RFA			3	–
A.S.C.			1	–
R.E.A. (HQ 2 Div)			1	–
Total	–	–	16	5
Other Divisions				
1 Brigade 1 Division	1[x]	–	–	–
2 Welsh R	–		1	–
Total	1		1	–

Evac'd by MAC.
Officers 2
O Ranks 15
Retd to duty
Officers 2
O Ranks 0
Retd to light duty
O Ranks 10

	Sick	Wnd
Adm'd Officers	1	–
" O Ranks	17	5
Evac'd Officers	2	1
" O Ranks	14	1
Remaining Officers	1	1
" O Ranks	57	26

Prevailing disease – Nil
No adm'd with foot trouble – one.
x Brig Genl H.C. LOWTHER 1 Bde 1 Div. N.Y.D.

A.S. Anderson

ADMS
2 Div
2/3/15.
9 am

Captn Lamb
for O.C. No 4 Field Amb

DHH

No 4 Field Ambulance.

Table showing No of Sick & Wound. admitted & [illegible] during 24 hours ending [illegible] 4/12/15

2 Division	Officers Sick	Officers Wound	Other Ranks Sick	Other Ranks Wound
2 Gren Gds	-	-	3	-
1 Irish "	-	-	1	-
2 HLI	-	1	-	3
9 HLI	-	-	1	-
RFA 41 Bde	1	0	1	-
Kings	-	-	1	-
1 Herts	-	-	1	-
Divl Signal att Staff	1	-	-	-
A.C.C.	-	-	1	-
A.S.C. 3rd	-	-	1	-
RAMC att 2 HLI	-	-	-	1
[illegible]	-	-	-	1
15 Hussars	1	-	-	-
TOTAL	3	1	10	5
Other D.				
1 S W B	1	-	-	-

[illegible]

Evac by MAC	
Officers	[illegible]
O Ranks	7
Ret to duty	
Officers	2
O Ranks	[illegible]
[illegible]	2

		Sick	Wound
Admitted	Officers	4	1
	O Ranks	10	5
Evacd	Officers	2	-
	O Ranks	2	5
Rems	Officers	11	
	O Ranks	38	26

2 Lt B B Murdoch RFA [illegible] NYD.
[illegible] 15 Hussars NYD
[illegible] D'Arcy [illegible] NYD
Capt F.C. Mackay 2 HLI [illegible]
[illegible] Stewart [illegible] 1 SWB NYD.

J S [illegible]

ADMS 2 Div
9 am
4/12/15

Capt Rowe
for OC No 4 Fd Amb.

No 4 Field Ambulance
Table showing No of Sick & Wounded by units admitted during 24 hours ending 5/3/15

	Officers Sick	Officers Wnded	O. Ranks Sick	O. Ranks Wnded
2 Coldm Gds	-	-	2	-
3 [illegible]	-	-	2	-
2 Grens	-	-	1	-
1 Irish	-	-	3	-
2 H.L.I.	-	-	—	[illegible]
1 Herts	-	-	1	[illegible]
1 K.R.R.	-	-	1	1
R.E. 5th Fld Co.	1	-	-	-
R.E. Sig. [illegible]	-	-	1	-
[illegible] R.H.A.	-	-	1	-
2 Innis Fus				1
Total	1	-	12	4

Other Divisions

1st Coldm Gds	1	-	-	-

Prevailing diseases: Diarrhoea
No of cases [illegible]

			Sick	W.
[illegible] by M.O.C. Officers		Admitted Officers	2	-
O.Ranks 15		O.Ranks	12	7
Retd to duty Officers 1		Evac. Officers	2	
		O.Ranks	10	6
O.Ranks 4		Remg Officers	10	2
[illegible] other ranks 1		O.Ranks	27	24

2nd Lt W. T. Scott-Elliott 1 Coldm Gds NYD
2 Lt R. M. Vibart R.E. 5th F. Co. NYD.

J S [illegible]

ADMS
2 Div
5.3.15
9 am

Capt. RAMC
f. O.C. No 4 Field Ambce

No 4 Field Ambulance

Table of Sick Wounded & Admitted during [illegible] ended 9 am 6/3/15

2nd Division		Officers Sick	Officers Wnd	Other Ranks Sick	Other Ranks Wnd
2 Cold Gds		—	—	3	—
2 Gren "		—	—	1	—
1 Irish "		—	—	4	—
2 Oxfords		—	—	—	1
2 S Staffs		—	—	—	1
1 H.L.I.		—	—	1	—
9 H.L.I.		—	—	1	—
R.E.		—	—	—	—
5th Bde R.F.A.		—	—	2	—
1 L.N. Lancs	1st Division	2×	—	—	—
TOTAL		2	—	13	2

Prevailing disease Influenza.
Good health

Evac'd by MAC	
Officers	3
O Ranks	12
Ret'd to Units	
Officers	1
O Ranks	4
Ret'd to L[illegible] Duty	
Other Ranks	4

		Sick	Wnd
Admitted	Officers	2	—
"	O Ranks	13	2
Evac'd	Officers	3	1
"	O Ranks	14	6
Remaining	Officers	9	1
"	O Ranks	37	19

Nil

× Capt. C Dare 1 L. Nth. Lancs Influenza
2 Lt. D.R. Curwen. — do — — do —

P.A.L.

L S [illegible]

Captn Raab
for OC. No 4 Field Amb

ADMS
2 Div
6/3/15
9 am.

78

No 4 Field Ambulance

Table showing No of sick + wound by units admitted during 24 hours ended 7/3/15

2 Division	Officers Sick	Wnd	O ranks Sick	Wnd
2 Colds	-	-	1	-
3 Colds	-	-	-	1
2 Grens	-	-	2	1
1 Irish	1 x	-	3	1
2 Oxfords	-	-	-	1
1 KRR	-	-	1	-
1 R Berks	-	-	-	1
ASC 11th Co	-	-	-	1
RE 5th Co	-	-	-	1
RGA 1 Siege Batty	-	-	1	1
1 Herts	-	-	2	-
	1	-	10	8
Other Divisions				
RE 26th Co	-	-	2	-

Prevailing disease - Bronchitis Catarrhal
No admd with foot trouble = Nil

				Sick	Wnd
Evacd by MAC		Admitted Officers		1	-
Officers	4	"	O Ranks	12	8
O Ranks	15	Evacuated Officers		3	1
Retd to duty		"	O Ranks	18	5
Officers	Nil	Remaining Officers		7	-
O Ranks	7	"	O Ranks	33	19
Retd to Lt duty 1					

x Lt T. G. Burke. 1st Irish Gds - Influenza

J S [illegible]

ADMS. 2 DW

9-am

7/3/15

Captn RAMC

for OC. No 4 Field Ambce

No 4 Field Ambulance
Table showing No of Sick & Wounded by units admitted during 24 hours ended 9 a.m. 8/3/15.

2 Division	Officers Sick	Officers Wd	O Ranks Sick	O Ranks Wd
2 Coldm Gds	-	-	1	-
3 Colds Gds	-	-	1	-
2 Gren Gds	-	+ -	2	-
1 Irish	1	-	2	-
2 Worcs	-	-	-	3
5 -do-	-	-	-	1
5 Kings	-	-	1	-
2 HLI	-	-	-	1
44 Bde RFA	-	-	2	-
1 M M G Sect	-	-	1	-
TOTAL	1	-	10	5
Other Divisions				
Unattached List. Indian Army attached 2 Munsters	-	1	-	-

Prevailing disease = Bronchitis Catarrh
No admitted with foot trouble. = 1.

Evacd by MAC	
Officers	1
O Ranks	6
Retd to duty	
Officers	1
Other Ranks	~~4~~
Retd to Lt duty	1

	Sick	Wd
Admitted Officers	1	1
" O Ranks	10	5
Evacuated Officers	2	-
" O Ranks	7	-
Remaining Officers	4	-
" O Ranks	37	23

+ Lt F C Blom. 1st Irish Gds. NYD.
2nd Lt E R S Dods. Unattached List } Bullet Wnd
~~ ~~ Indian Army } R Upper Arm
att 2 Munsters

J S Dunn

Capt Lamb
for O.C. No 4 Fld Amb

ADMS
2 Div 9 a.m
8 3 15

No 4 Field Ambulance

Table showing no. of [illegible] admitted by units [illegible] during [illegible] ended 9/3/15.

2 Division				
3 Cold. Gds	1		1	
3 [illegible] "			1	
2 Gren. "			2	
1 Herts			2	
R F A [illegible] Bde			4	
3 Kings			1	
R E 2nd Sig Co			1	
2 Innis. Fus	1			
Total	2	—	12	—
Other Divisions				
2 Sussex	1	—	—	—
1 Black Watch	1			
Total	2	—	—	—

					Sick	Wound
Enc. [illegible]	[illegible] admitted [illegible]					
Officers	—	—	Admitted	Officers	4	—
O Ranks		11	"	O Ranks	12	—
Rest & Duty			Evac.	Officers	2	—
Officers		2	"	O Ranks	25	2
Other Units		8	Remaining	Officers	8	1
Retd to Duty		8		O Ranks	27	18

Lt E.K. Stevenson 1 Cold. Gds Influenza.
Lt C.H. Daniels 2 Innis. Fus. Influenza.
Lt A.C. Caddney 2/ Sussex [illegible]
Lt R K Campbell 1st Black Watch [illegible].

PMA

J S [illegible]
Captn RAMC
for OC No 4 Field Ambce

ADMS
1 Div

9.3.15

No 4 Field Ambulance

Table showing number of Sick & Wounded by units admitted during 24 hours ended 11/3/15

2 Division	Officers Sick	Officers Wnd	Other ranks Sick	Other ranks Wnd
2 Gren Gds	.	.	1	.
1 Irish Gds	1	.	1	2
1 KRR	.	1	.	74
1 Kings Lpool	.	2	.	58
5 do do	.	.	.	3
2 Sth Staffs	.	4	.	37
2 Worcs	1	.	.	4
1 R Berks	.	.	.	4
2 Innis Fus	.	.	.	3
2 HLI	.	.	.	3
9 HLI	.	.	.	1
RE 5th Fld Co	.	.	.	2
RE (Rest A.Q)	1	.	.	4
1 Scotch Gds	.	1	.	.
ASC 2 Div	.	1	1	.
2 Gren Gds att'd Scotch Gds	.	1	.	.
Total	3	9	3	195
Other Divisions				
London Scottish	1	.	.	.
4 R Welsh Fus	.	1	.	.
5 R Sussex	1	.	.	.
RE 26th Co	.	.	1	.
	2	1	1	.

Prevailing disease Nil
Foot Troubles Nil

Evac'd by MAC
Officers 12
O Ranks 160
Ret'd to duty
Officers Nil
Other Ranks 3
Ret'd to T. duty 10

		Sick	Wnd
admitted	Officers	5	10
	O Ranks	4	195
Evac'd	Officers	3	9
	O Ranks	33	140
Remained	Officers	13	1
"	O Ranks	12	53

PLJ

A.D.M.S.
2 Div
9 am
11-3-15

P A Lloyd Jones
Capt RAMC
O.C. No 4 Fld Ambce

1 Nominal roll of officers admitted yesterday. (10 3 15)

Lt. L.R. YEO. 2 Sth Staffs B Wound Abdomen died 10/3/15
2nd Lt. RICHARDSON 2 Sth Staffs G.S.W. Head.
Lieut. T.S. TOWNSEND 2 Sth Staffs G.S.W. L Shoulder Head
Lieut. C. CORNOCK-TAYLOR London Scottish
2nd Lieut. L. STRAKER 1st Irish Gds
2 Lieut. A.A.B. DEWING 5 R Sussex
Lt. A.T. BERRY R E (East Ang)
2nd Lt. J.D. WILLMOT. 2nd Worcs.
Lt. P.C. SNATT 1st Kings Lpool B Wound L Thigh
Major B.N. ROMILLY 1st Scotch Gds. Shell wound Head
Lt. A.D.P. KINGSMILL 2 Gren Gds att 1 Scotch Gds Shell Wd Head
2nd Lt. H. ELSE 1st K.R.R. B Wound R Ankle
2nd Lt. R.P. WARD 4th R Welsh Fus B Wound Head Hand
Col. VC M. CARTER. 1st Kings Lpool G.S.W. Shldr
2 Lt. A.D. Sprint. 2 Sth Staffs Shell Wound Back

PHJ

ADMS
7 Div
11.3.15

P. A. Lloyd Jones
Capt RAMC
OC. No 4 Field Ambulance

No. 4 Field Ambulance

Table shewing No. of Sick admitted by Units admitted during 24 hours ended 12/3/[illegible] (9 am)

2 Division	Officers Sick	Officers Wound^d	O Ranks Sick	O Ranks Wound^d
3 Coldstream Gds				1
2 Grenadier "	1		1	3
1 Irish "	1		1	3
1 Kings			1	7
1 KRR			2	8
1 R Berks			2	2
~~[illegible]~~			-	~~2~~
2 Sth Staffs			-	6
R E 11th Co.			1	
5 Kings			5	1
Herts			1	-
RFA 44 Bde			1	-
A.C.C. 2 Div			3	-
Total	2	-	18	28
Other Divisions				
1 Coldstream Gds	1	-	-	-
1 Black Watch		1		
Total	1	1	-	-

Prevailing disease :- Nil
Foot troubles adm^d :- Nil

Evac^d by MAC	
Officers	4
O Ranks	63
Ret^d to duty	
Officers	Nil
O Ranks	Nil
Ret^d to [illegible] duty	Nil

		Sick	Wound^d
Admitted	Officers	3	1
"	O Ranks	18	28
Evac^d	Officers	1	3
"	O Ranks	3	60
Remain^g	Officers	13	1
"	O Ranks	26	25

Capt E D RIDLEY 2nd Gren^r Gds. N.Y.D.
Capt E.B. GREER 1 Irish Gds N.Y.D.
Lieut Hon. C NOEL 1 Colds Gds N.Y.D.
2Lt J.W. Garden 1 Black Watch Wound Heart.

P. H. Lloyd Jones

ADMS
2 Div
9 am
12. 3. 15.

Capt RAMC
OC No 4 Field Amb^ce

No. 4 Field Ambulance

No. of sick and wounded admitted, by Units, during 24 hours ended 9 am. 13/3/15.

Units. 2nd Division	Officers Sick	Officers Wnd	Other Ranks Sick	Other Ranks Wnd
2nd Gren Gds.	–	–	–	1
2nd Coldstream Gds.	–	–	2	–
3rd Coldstream Gds.	–	–	1	1
1st. Irish Guards	~~1~~	–	1	4
1st. Herts (T)	–	–	3	2
1st. R. Berks.	–	–	7	–
1st. K.R.R.	–	–	–	1
1st. Kings.	–	–	3	–
2nd H.L.I.	1	–	–	–
2nd S. Staffs.	–	–	3	–
R.F.A. 50th. Batty	–	–	2	–
R.G.A. 26th. Hy Batty	–	–	1	–
No1. Batty M.M.G. Sec.	–	–	2	–
~~[illegible]~~	~~1~~	–		
3rd Somersets att. K.R.R.	2	–		
Total.	~~5~~ 4	–	25	9
Other Divisions:				
R.F.A. 115 Batty.	1	–	–	–

Evac^d by M.A.C.
Officers – 6
Other Rks. 22
Ret^d to duty:
Officers 1
Other Rks. 10
Ret^d to L.n. duty
Other Rks. Nil.

Prevailing Disease – Bronchitis Catarrh
No. admitted with foot Troubles. Nil

		Sick	Wnd.
Admitted	Officers	5	–
"	Other Rks.	25	9
Evac^d.	Officers	7	–
"	Other Rks.	11	17.
Remaining.	Officers.	11	2.
"	Other Rks.	41	17.

Lieut G.E.W. FRANKLYN, R.F.A. 115 Batty, Suspected Enteric.
~~" W. DOWSE, R.A.M.C. att. 3 K.R.R. [illegible]~~
2 Lieut. D.W. GUNSTON, 1st. Irish Guards, Gastritis
Lieut. B. CROSSLEY, 2nd. H.L.I., Bronchitis
" S.J. STEADMAN, 3rd. Somerset att. 1 K.R.R., Shock.
" C.E. BIRKETT, —do— Shock

R.A. Lloyd Jones
Capt. RAMC
OC. No. 4 Fd. Amb.

ADMS. 2nd Divn
13/3/15

No. 4 Field Ambulance

No of sick and wounded admitted, by Units, during 24 hours ended 9 a.m. 14/3/15.

Unit. 2nd Divn	Officers Sick	Officers wounded	Other Sick	Ranks. wounded.
2nd Grenadier Guards	–	–	–	1
2nd Coldstream "	–	–	1	2
1st Herts.	–	–	–	2
1st 5th Kings	–	–	1	–
1st R. B.	–	–	4	–
1st. K. R.	–	–	1	1
2nd ~~Oxford~~ K.R.R.	1	–	–	1
2nd H. L. I.	–	–	–	1
9th. H. L. I.	–	–	–	1
7th. Kings.	–	–	1	–
R. E. 5th Fd Coy.	–	–	1	–
R. G. A. No. 7. Mtn Batty.	–	1	–	–
Total.	1	1	9	9
2nd Division				
5th. Gurkhas.	–	1	–	–
3 London ~~Scottish~~ Regt.	–	1	–	–

Prevailing Disease Nil.
No. with foot troubles Nil.

		Sick	Wndd.
Admitted	Officers	1	3
"	Other Rks.	9	9
Evac'd	Officers	6	1
"	Other Rks.	14	6
Remng.	Officers	7	3
"	Other Rks.	36	20.

Evac'd by M.A.C.
Officers. 1
Other Rks. 10
To Duty.
Officers 6
Other Rks. 5
To Light Duty.
Other Rks. 5.

Lieut A. R. MOORE, 3rd London Regt. Shell wnd L. Thigh
" H. R. H. ROUQUETTE R.G.A., No 7. Mn. Batt. Bullet wnd L. Shdr.
Maj C. E. BATEMAN-CHAMPAIN, 5th Gurkhas, " " Chest.
Lieut. R. T. Sherlock, 2nd K.R.R., N.Y.D.

P. H. Lloyd Jones.
Capt. RAMC
O.C. No. 4 Fd. Amb.

A.D.M.S. 2nd Divn
14/3/15.

No. 4 Field Ambulance

No.s of sick and wounded, by Units, admitted during 24 hours ended 9am. 1-3/15.

Unit 2nd Divis.	Officers Sick	Officers Wnded.	Other Rks. Sick	Other Rks. Wnded
2nd Grenadier Guards.	–	–	–	5
2nd Coldstream "	–	–	1	4
3rd Coldstream "	–	–	3	–
1st Irish Guards.	–	–	1	–
1st Herts.	–	–	1	4
1st K. R. R.	–	–	–	1
1st R. Berks.	–	–	8	–
1st 5th. Kings.	–	–	2	–
2nd 5th. Staffs.	–	–	1	–
R. G. A. 1st Sge Batty.	–	–	2	–
R. F. A. 50th. Batty.	–	–	1	–
R. F. A. 70th. Batty.	–	–	1	–
A. C. C. 2nd Divn.	–	–	1	–
2nd H. L. I.	1	–	–	–
Totals.	1	–	22	14
Other Divisions.				
1st Queens.	–	–	2	–
4th R. W. Fus.ns	1	–	–	–
2nd R Sussex	1	–	–	–
Totals.	2	–	2	–

Prevailing Disease Bronchitis Catarrh
No. with foot troubles. 1.

		Sick	Wnd.
Admitted	Officers.	3	–
"	Other Rks.	24	14
Evac'd.	Officers.	4	2
	Other Rks.	28	14
Remng.	Officers	6	1
"	Other Rks.	32	19

Evac'd. M. A. C.
Officers. 4
Other Rks. 33
Ret'd duty
Officers 2
Other Rks. 4
Ret'd light duty 5.

Lieut. R. A. F. WHISTLER, 2nd H. L. I. N. Y. D.
" O. AUSTIN, 2nd R. Sussex N. Y. D.
2nd Lt. D. C. JOHNSON 4th. R. W. Fus.rs Shock.

A.D.M.S. 2nd Divn

P. A. Lloyd Jones
Capt. RAMC
O.C. No. 4 Fd. Amce

No. 4 Field Ambulance

No of Sick and wounded admitted, by Units, during 24 hours ended 9am. 16/3/15.

Units 2nd Divn.	Officers. Sick	Officers. Wndd.	Other Rks. Sick	Other Rks. Wndd.
2nd Grenadier Guards.	–	–	4	–
2nd Coldstream "	–	–	4	3
3rd Coldstream "	–	–	–	1
1st Irish Guards.	–	–	2	5
1st Herts.	–	–	1	3
1st. K.R.R.	–	–	–	2
1st. R. Berks.	–	–	1	–
1st. Kings.	–	–	2	1
1st 5th Kings	–	–	3	–
2nd S. Staffs.	–	–	2	–
9th H.L.I.	–	–	2	–
R.F.A. 15th Batty.	–	1	–	–
" 47th "	–	–	1	–
59th Rifles	–	1	–	–
1st. H.L.I.	–	1	–	–
R.E. 5th Fd. Co.	–	–	1	–
A.C.C.	–	–	1	–
Totals.	–	3	24	15
Other Divns.				
4th. Suffolks.	1	–	–	–
	1	–	–	–

Prevailing Disease – Bronchitis Catarrh
No. with foot troubles. 2.

Evac. M.A.C.
Officers – 4
Other Rks. 23
Retd Duty –
Officers 1
Other Rks. 4
Retd Light Duty –
Other Rks. 6

		Sick	Wndd
Admitted	Officers	1	3
"	Other Rks.	24	15
Evac'd	Officers	3	2
	Other Rks.	20	13
Remaining	Officers	4	2
"	Other Rks.	36	20

Capt. B.L. MARRINER R.F.A., 15th. Batty, Bullet wnd L. Arm
" J.A. KNIGHT, 1st. H.L.I., Shell wnd R. Arm & Leg.
" R.D. INSKIP 59th. Rifles, " " L. Arm.
" H.D. MITCHELL, 4th Suffolks, Shock.
Brig. Gen F C CARTER 24th. Infty Bde N.Y.D.

ADMS 2nd Divn
16/3/15.

[illegible]
Capt RAMC.
OC 4th Fd Amb

No. 4 Field Ambulance.

No. of sick and wounded admitted during 24 hours ended 9 am 17/8/15

Unit – 2nd Div.	Officers Sick	Officers Wndd.	Other Ranks Sick	Other Ranks Wndd.
2nd Grenadier Guards.	–	–	–	2
2nd Coldstream "	1	–	1	1
3rd Coldstream "	–	–	3	3
1st Irish Guards.	–	–	–	2
1st Herts.	–	–	–	4
1st Kings.	–	–	–	1
1st R. Berks.	–	–	2	–
2nd. S. Staffs.	–	–	4	–
R.F.A. 15th Batty.	–	1	–	–
44th Bde.	–	–	2	–
R.E. 5th Fd. Coy.	–	–	–	1
Totals.	1	1	12	14
Other Divs.				
1st Scots Guards.	1	–	–	–
R.F.A. 81st Batty	–	1	–	–
" 52nd "	1	–	–	–
Totals.	2	1	–	–

Prevailing Disease – Nil.
No. with foot troubles. Nil.

		Sick	Wndd.
Admitted	Officers	3	2
"	Other Rks.	12	14
Evac'd	Officers	2	3
	Other Rks.	10	16
Remaining	Officers	5	1
"	Other Rks.	38	16

Evac'd M.A.C.
Officers – 5
Other Rks. – 15
Retd to Duty –
Officers –
Other Rks. 8
Retd Regt Duty
Other Rks. 3

Lieut. P. WRIGHT, R.F.A. 15th Batty, Bullet wnd { Head & L. Hand
" E.D. MACKENZIE, 1st Scots Gds. Pharyngitis
2nd Lt. J. SMITH, R.F.A. 81st Batty Shell wnd. Leg.
" S.H. HALL, " 54th " N.Y.D.
Lieut. D.E. TRAFFORD, 2nd Colds. Gds. Constipation

P. A. Lloyd Neck

A.D.M.S. 2nd Divn.
17/8/15.

OC. 4th Fd. Ambce.

No. 4 Field Ambulance.

No. of sick and wounded, by units, admitted during 24 hours ended 9 a.m. 15/3/15.

Unit and Division	Officers Sick	Officers Wounded	Other Ranks Sick	Other Ranks Wounded
2nd [illegible]	–	–	1	8
2nd [illegible]	–	–	2	1
2nd [illegible]	–	–	2	3
1st [illegible]	–	–	–	3
1st [illegible]	–	–	2	–
1st [illegible]	–	–	1	–
[illegible]	–	–	[illegible]	1
[illegible] C.	–	–	3	–
[illegible]	–	–	2	–
1st [illegible] att. R.E. [illegible] Co.	1	–	–	–
Totals	1	–	13	16
Other Divisions: London Scottish, 4th Kings, 1st Manchesters, 59 Scinde Rifles, 4th Suffolks, 1st Queens	1, 1, 1, 1, 1, 1	/	/	–, 1
	6	–		1

[illegible]: Nil.
No. with foot troubles - Nil.

Evacuated by M.A.C.:-
Officers - 1
Other Ras - 23
Returned duty:-
Officers -
Other Ras - 7
[illegible]:-
Officers -
Other Ras - 3

	Sick	Wounded
Admitted officers	7	–
Other Ras.	13	17
[illegible] Officers	1	–
Other Ras.	24	9
Remaining officers	11	1
Other Ras.	27	22

Lieut. C. P. EDGECOMBE, [illegible] R.E. [illegible] Co. [illegible]

Major. J. H. LANG-SIMS, 4th Kings.
Capt. E. N. BUCHAN, 1st Manchesters.
Lieut. J. M. SCOBIE, 59th Scinde Rifles.
2nd Lt. G. W. STIBBINGS, 4th. Suffolks.
Lieut. J. B. CLOSE, 1st. Queens.
2nd Lt. R. A. MARSHALL, London Scottish.

} Bronchitis, [illegible], Contusions of [illegible]

P. A. Lloyd Jones
Capt. RAMC.
OC No. 4 Fd. Amb.

A.D.M.S. 2nd Divn
15/3/15.

No. 4 Field Ambulance

No. of sick and wounded by Units, admitted during 24 hours ended 9 a.m. 19/3/15.

2nd Divn. Unit	Officers Sick	Officers Wndd.	Other Ranks Sick	Other Ranks Wndd.
2nd Grenadier Guards.	–	1	–	1
2nd Coldstream "	–	–	1	3
1st. Herts.	–	–	1	1
1st. R. Berks.	–	–	4	–
1st. Kings.	–	–	1	–
2nd Worces.	–	–	–	1
2nd K. R. R.	–	–	–	1
ASC. 11th. Co.	–	–	1	–
ACC.	–	–	1	–
~~[illegible]~~				
Totals.	–	1	9	7
Other Divs.				
1st. Divnl. Artillery.	–	1	–	–
11th. Mdsex.	1	–	–	–
Totals.	1	1	–	–

Prevailing Disease – Nil.
No. with foot troubles.

Evac'd by M.A.C.
Officers – 1
Other Rks. 15
Retd duty
Officers – 1
Other Rks. 6
Retd light duty –
Other Rks. 3

		Sick	Wndd.
Admitted	officers	1	2
"	Other Rks.	9	7
Evac'd	officers	2	–
"	Other Rks.	24	12
Remaining	officers	10	3
"	Other Rks.	22	16

Capt. E. A. TRAFFORD, 11th. Mdsex, att 5th Rfls. Shock
Major H. A. RAMSEY, Bde. Maj. 1st Dvn. Artilly. G.S.W. Thigh.
" V. VIVIAN, Gren. Gds. Bde. Maj. 4th Gds. Bde. G.S.W. foot.

P. D. Lloyd Jones
Capt. RAMC
OC. No. 4 Fd. Amb.

ADMS. 2nd Dvn.
19/3/15.

No 4 Field Ambulance.

No of sick and wounded, by units, admitted during 24 hours ended 20/3/15.

Unit. 2nd Division.	Officers Sick	Officers Wndd	Other Rks. Sick	Other Rks. Wndd
3rd Coldstream Guards	–	–	1	–
1st Irish Guards.	–	–	1	4
1st Herts.	–	–	1	4
1st R Berks	–	–	2	–
1st Kings.	–	–	1	–
1st 5th Kings.	–	–	1	–
2nd Inniskg Fus	–	–	–	1
2nd S. Staffs.	–	–	–	1
A V Corps (No 3 mobile)	–	–	1	–
R E (East Anglian)	–	–	1	2
R E (Hd Qrs)	–	–	1	–
A S C (" ")	–	–	1	–
R A M C (No 4 Fd Amb).	–	–	1	–
Total	–	–	12	12
Other Divs.				
1st M'chesters.	1	–	–	–
~~[illegible]~~				
20th Fd Amb. (I M S)	–	–	1	–
Total	1	–	1	–

Prevailing Disease Nil
No with foot troubles. Nil.

Evac'd M. A. C.
Officers 1
Other Rks. 11
Ret'd Duty.
Officers 2
Other Rks. –
Ret'd Lt. Duty.
Other Rks. 2

		Sick	Wnd.
Admitted	Officers	1	–
	Other Rks	13	12
Evac'd	Officers	2	1
	Other Rks	2	9
Remaining	Officers	9	2
	Other Rks.	31	19.

Lieut. A. H. V. MOORE, 1st M'chester Regt. Shock.

ADMS. 2nd Divn
20/3/15.

[illegible] Capt. RAMC.
No. 4 Fd. Ambulance.

No. 4 Field Ambulance.

No. of sick and wounded, by units, admitted during 24 hours ended 9 am. 21/3/15.

Unit – 2nd Divn.	Officers Sick	Officers Wndd.	Other Rks Sick	Other Rks Wndd.
2nd Coldstream Guards.	–	–	–	1
1st. Irish Guards	1	–	1	–
1st. Herts.	–	–	3	1
1st. Kings.	1	–	–	–
1st. R. Berks.	–	–	6	–
7th. Kings	–	–	–	1
2nd S. Staffs.	–	–	2	–
2nd H. L. I.	–	–	–	2
R. F. A. 34th Bde.	–	–	1	–
" 36th "	–	–	1	–
" 56th Batty.	–	–	1	–
Total.	2	–	15	5
Other Divisions.				
4th City of London	–	1	–	–
2nd R. Muns. Fus.rs.	1	–	–	–
1st. Gurkha Rifles	1	–	–	–
Total.	2	1	–	–

Prevailing Disease None.
No. with foot troubles. 4

Evac. M. A. C.
Officers – 2
Other Rks. 17
Retd to Duty.
Officers –
Other Rks. 1
Retd Light Duty.
Other Rks. 1

	Sick	Wndd.
Admitted Officers	4	1
" Other Rks.	15	5
Evac'd Officers	1	1
" Other Rks.	12	7
Remg. Officers.	12	2
" Other Rks.	34	16

Major The Earl of Rosse, 1st. Irish Guards – Bron. Catarrh.
2nd Lt. J. S. RICH, 1st. Kings, Catarrhal Jaundice.
Lieut. T. T. SYKES, 4th City of London, G. S. W. Arm.
" J. A STEWART, 4th R. Muns. Fus. Influenza.
" W. St. J. CARPENDALE, 1st Gurkha Rifles. N. Y. D. Pyrexia.

P. A. Lloyd Jones
Capt. RAMC
OC. No. 4 Fd. Ambce.

ADMS. 2nd Divn.
21/3/15.

No. 4 Field Ambulance.

No. of Sick and wounded by Units, admitted during 24 hours ended 9am. 22/3/15.

Unit. 2nd Div.	Officers. Sick	Officers. Wndd.	Other Ranks. Sick	Other Ranks. Wndd.
2nd Grenadier Guards	–	–	2	7.
2nd Coldstream "	2	1	–	1
3rd Coldstream "	–	–	–	2
1st Irish Gds "	–	–	–	1
1st Herts.	–	–	1	–
1st K. R. R.	–	–	1	–
2nd S. Staffs.	1	–	–	–
A.S.C.	–	–	2	–
2nd K. R. R.	–	1	–	–
A. C. C.	–	–	1	–
5th. Kings.	–	–	4	–
2nd H. L. I.	–	–	1	–
R. F. A. (M. M. G.)	–	–	1	–
R. F. A.	–	–	1	–
R. G. A. 1st. Sge Batt.	–	–	1	–
3rd Warwicks att. 1 R. Berks.	1	–	–	–
Totals.	4	2	15	11
Other Divs.				
1st. Black Watch.	1	–	–	–
RAMC (att 1 H.L.I.)	–	1	–	–
Totals.	1	1	–	–

Prevailing Disease. – None.
No. with foot troubles. None.

		Sick	Wndd.
Admitted	Officers	5	3
	Other Rks.	15	11
Evac'd	Officers	7	1
"	Other Rks.	8	9.
Remaining	Officers	9	5
"	Other Rks.	40	18.

Evac'd M.A.C.
Officers – 8
Other Rks. 14

Ret'd duty.
Officers Nil
Other Rks. 1. (A.S.C. 2nd H.Q.)

Ret'd light duty 3. { R. F. A. / 1st Kings / 1st R. Berks. }

2nd Lt. H. DRAYCOTT-WOOD, 2nd S. Staffs. Pyorrhoea Alveolaris
Lieut. L. C. RATTRAY, 2nd Kings. G.S.W. Scalp.
Capt. J. S. EGERTON, 2nd Colds. Neurasthenia.
2. Lt. J. T. SHUTE, 3rd Warwicks, att. 1 R Berks. Internal derangement knee.
" H. H. BURNS, 2nd Colds. Gds. Influenza.
" R. M. PURVIS, 1st. Black Watch, Otitis media.
Lieut. MACKENZIE, RAMC. att. 1st H.L.I. Shell wnd L. Arm.
Capt. E. G. GREGGE-HOPWOOD, 2nd Colds. Bullet wnd Face.

A.D.M.S. 2nd Divn

P. A. Lloyd Jones
Capt. RAMC
O.C. 4th F. Amb.

No. 6 Field Ambulance

No. of sick and wounded, by units, admitted during 24 hours ended 9 a.m. 23/3/15.

Unit – 2nd Division.	Officers. Sick	Officers. Wndd.	Other Rks. Sick	Other Rks. Wndd.
2nd Grenadier Guards.	–	–	1	4
2nd Coldstream	–	–	1	–
1st. Herts.	–	–	–	1
7th. Kings.	–	1	–	–
R.E. 5th. F Coy.	–	–	1	–
R.G.A. 26th Batty.	–	–	1	–
R.F.A. 34th Bde.	–	–	1	–
R.E. 2nd Div. Sigs.	–	–	2	–
K.O.S.B. att. 2. H.L.I.	1	–	1	–
Totals.	1	1	7	5
Other Divs.				
57th. Suffolk Reg. (German)	–	–	–	1
15th. Hussars.	2	–	–	–
2nd R. Sussex	1	–	–	–
5th. R. Sussex.	1	–	–	–
125 Napiers Rifles.	1	–	–	–
R.E. 21. Sig. Co.	1	–	–	–
Totals.	6	–	–	1

Prevailing disease Nil
No. with foot troubles. Nil.

Evac. M.A.C.
Officers 5
Other Rks. 17
Ret'd Duty
Officers 1 (54th Batt R.F.A.).
Other Rks 3 (1, R.F.A. [illegible] Bde, [illegible]
Ret'd Light duty [illegible], 1, 5th Kings).
Other Rks. 4 (1, 6th Kings, 2, 1 R. Berks, 1, 1st Herts.).

	Sick	Wndd.
Admitted officers.	7	1
Other Rks.	7	6
Evac'd officers.	5	1
Other Rks.	17	7
Remaining. Officers.	11	5
Other Rks.	30	17.

Lieut. P.P. CURTIS, XV Hussars, Measles.
" H.H. JACKSON, " Sprain Ankle.
Capt. H.S. ASHWORTH 2nd R. Sussex, Contusion foot.
" A.E.D. ANDERSON, K.O.S.B. att. 2. H.L.I. Inflammation Tonsils
2nd Lt. C.R.C. SMITH 7th. Kings Shell wind chest (slight).
Lieut. M. FITZMAURICE, R.E. 21st. Co. Mumps.
" J.B. AITON, 5th. R. Sussex, Bronchitis Catarrhal.
Capt. C.H. STEVENSON, 125th Napier Rfls. N.Y.D. Influenza.

[illegible]
Capt R.A.M.C.
oc No. 6 Fd. Ambce

A.D.M.S. 2nd Divn

23/3/15.

No. 4 Field Ambulance.

No. of sick and wounded, by Units, admitted during 24 hours ended 24/3/15.

Unit – 2nd Divn	Officers Sick	Officers Wndd	Other Rks. Sick	Other Rks. Wndd	Remarks.*
2nd Coldstream Guards.	1	–	1	3	Ret'd Lt. Duty
1st Irish Gds.	–	–	2	4	
1st Herts.	–	–	1	2	
2nd S. Staffs.	1	–	4	–	1 R. Berks. 4
5th Kings.	–	1	–	–	1 Herts. 1.
7th Kings.	–	–	1	–	R.F.A. [illegible]
R.E. 2nd Fd Co.	–	–	1	–	2. S. Staffs. 1.
R.F.A. 44th Bde.	–	–	2	1	5th Kings 1.
R.F.A. 70th Batty.	–	–	1	–	
ACC. 2nd Div.	–	–	3	–	
A.V.C. 3 Mobile.	–	–	1	–	
Total.	2	1	17	10	8

Prevailing Disease. Nil

No. with foot troubles. Nil

	Sick	Wndd.
Admitted Officers	2	1
" Other Rks.	17	10
Evac'd Officers.	3	–
Other Rks.	24	6
Remaining Officers.	10	6
Other Rks.	23	21.

Evac'd by M.A.C.
Officers – 2
Other Rks. 22
Ret'd to Duty.
Officers 1 Scots Gds.
Other Rks. Nil.
Ret'd Light Duty
Other Rks. 18.*

Lieut. B. BIRBECK, 2nd Colds. Gds. Influenza.
" T.H.R. EVANS, 2nd S. Staffs, Hydrocele.
" N.K. MACDONALD, 6th. Kings, Shell wnd Face.

[signature]

Capt. RAMC
OC. No. 4 Fd. Amb.

A.D.M.S. 2nd Divn
24/3/15. 9 am.

No. 4 Field Ambulance.

No. of sick and wounded by Units, admitted during 24 hours ended 9am. 25/3/15.

Unit – 2nd Divn.	Officers Sick	Officers Wndd.	Other Rks. Sick	Other Rks. Wndd	Remarks.
2nd Grenadier Guards.	–	–	–	1	Officers Retd duty.
1st. Irish Guards.	–	1	–	–	1 Irish Gds (Convalesc).
1st. Herts.	–	–	2	–	1 2 Colds. "
2nd S. Staffs.	–	–	1	–	1 2 H.R.R.
					Other Rks to duty.
2nd Kings	–	1	–	–	1. R.F.A. M.M.G.
9th. H.L.I.	–	–	–	1	1. R.S. 5th Fd. Co.
A.C.C.	–	–	1	–	
Totals.	–	2	4	2	3. Officers 2 other Rks.
Other Divs.					
1st. S.W. Borderers.	–	–	1	–	Other Rks to Light duty
4th R.W. Fusiliers	–	–	1	–	
1st. Coldstream Gds.	1	–	–	–	1. 5th Kings.
1st. Connaught Rang.	1	–	–	–	1. 1st. R. Berks.
1st Irish Gds. att. 1 Scots Gd.	1	–	–	–	2. 2nd Colds. Gds.
1st L.N. Lancs.	1	–	–	–	1. A.S.C.
Totals	4	–	2	–	5 to Light duty.

Prevailing Disease – Nil
Admitted with foot troubles Nil.

Evac'd by M.A.C. –
Officers – 2
Other Rks – 12
Retd to Duty: –
Officers – 3
Other Rks – 2
Retd Light duty: –
Other Rks – 5

		Sick	Wnd.
Admitted	Officers	4	2
"	Other Rks.	6	2
Evac'd	Officers	3	2
"	Other Rks.	13	6
Remaining	Officers	11	6
"	Other Rks.	16	15

Lieut. W. H. OCKLESTON, 5th Kings Shell wnd L. Shoulder.
2nd Lt. T. A. TAPP, 1st. Coldstr. Guards, Enteritis
" " W. T. F. LATHAM, 1st. Conn. Rangers, Bronchitis Catarrhal.
Lieut. D. C. PARSONS, 1st. Irish, att 1st. Scots. Gds. Influenza.
2nd Lt. T. FAWDRY, 1st L. N. Lancs, Neurasthenia.
" " T. E. G. NUGENT, 1st. Irish Gds. Bullet wnd Neck.

P. A. Lloyd Jones
Capt. RAMC
OC. No. 4 Fd. Ambce.

A.D.M.S. 2nd Divn.
25/3/15.

[illegible] 24 [illegible] 26/3/15.

[illegible]	Officers Sick	Officers Wounded	Other Ranks Sick	Other Ranks Wounded	Remarks.
[illegible]	–	–	–	2	Officers to Duty
[illegible]	–	–	2	–	2nd R. Sussex.
[illegible] Guards.	–	–	–	1	
[illegible]	–	–	1	1	
[illegible]	–	1	–	–	Other Rks to Light Duty
[illegible] Staffs.	–	–	4	–	
R. [illegible]	–	–	–	1	1, 3 Colds. Gds.
[illegible] Bat.	–	–	1	–	1, 2. S. Staffs.
[illegible] Bat.	–	–	1	–	
[illegible] H.Q.	–	–	1	–	
R.E. 26th Coy.	–	1,	–	–	
2. Oxfords → Total.	–	3	10	5	
[illegible]					
[illegible] Div.	1	–	–	–	
[illegible] City of London	–	1	–	–	
Total.	1	1	–	–	

[illegible] Nil.
[illegible] 1.

[illegible] M.A.C.
[illegible] 5
[illegible] 9
[illegible]
[illegible] 1
Other Rks. Nil.
[illegible] duty
Other Rks. 2.

		[illegible]	[illegible]
[illegible]	Officers	1	4
	Other Rks.	10	5
[illegible]	Officers	2	4
	Other Rks.	4	7
[illegible]	Officers	10	6
	Other Rks.	22	11.

[illegible] C EILLS, [illegible] Kings, [illegible]
[illegible] E. GORE-BROWN, [illegible] City of London, [illegible]
[illegible] W. G. HIGGINS, [illegible]
2 Lt. C. R. HORLEY, 2nd Oxfords. G.S.W. R. Foot.
~~R.E.~~
2nd Lt. E. ~~B~~ W. RUSE, R.E. 26th Co. G.S.W. Buttocks.

P. A. Lloyd Jones
Capt. R.A.M.C.
O.C. No. 4 Fd. Amb.

[illegible] 2nd Div.
26/3/15.

1

No. 4 Field Ambulance
No of sick and wounded admitted by Units, during 24 hours ended 9 am. 27/3/15.

Unit. 2nd Divn.	Officers Sick	Officers Wndd.	Other Ranks Sick	Other Ranks Wndd.	Remarks.
2nd Grenadier Guards	–	–	2	2	Officers to duty
1st. Herts.	–	–	–	1	1 London Scott.
2nd Coldstream Guards	–	–	–	1	1 K.O.S.B.
1st. Kings.	–	1	–	–	1 125 Napiers Rifles
1/5th. Kings	–	–	1	–	
Totals.	–	1	3	4	3.
Other Divs.					Other Rks. to light duty
1R.F.A. 94th Batt.	–	–	1	–	
6th London.	–	–	1	–	2. A.C.C.
5th City of London	–	–	1	–	1. A.V.C.
R.F.A. 113 Batty.	–	–	1	–	1 R.E.
A.S.C. No. 1 Am. Pk.	1	–	–	–	
1st. Black Watch	1	–	–	–	
Totals.	2	–	4	–	4.

Prevailing Disease – Nil
No. with foot troubles – Nil.

		Sick	Wndd
Admitted	Officers	2	1
"	Other Rks.	7	4
Evac'd	Officers	4	3
	Other Rks.	14	–
Remng.	Officers	8	2
"	Other Rks.	15	15

Evac'd by M.A.C.
Officers 6
Other Rks. 10
Retd. to duty,
Officers 3
Other Rks. Nil
Retd. to light duty.
Other Rks 4.

2nd Lt. H.V. TRUBSHAWE, 1st. Kings, G.S.W. R. Wrist.
" " J.S.O. ELLISON, A.S.C., M.T. Bronchitis Catarrhal.
Lieut. WANLISS, 1st. Black Watch, Enteritis

P. A. Lloyd Jones
Capt. RAMC.
O.C. No 4 Fd. Amb.

ADMS. 2nd Divn.
27/3/15

No. 4 Field Ambulance.

No. of sick and wounded admitted, by Units, during 24 hours ended 9am. 28/3/15.

Unit – 2nd Division	Officers Sick	Officers Wndd.	Other Rks. Sick	Other Rks. Wndd.	Remarks.
2nd Coldstream Gds.	–	–	–	1	Officers to Duty
1st. Irish Guards.	–	–	–	2	1. 5th. R. Sussex.
1st. Herts.	–	–	–	2	1. 1st. Colds. Gds.
1st K.R.R.	–	–	3	–	Other Rks. Duty.
2nd Innisky. Fusrs.	–	–	–	1	
R.F.A. (7th M.G. Sec.)	–	–	1	–	1. 6th City of London. 1. 2nd S. Staffs.
" 56th. Batty.	–	–	1	–	Other Rks. Lt. Duty 1. Herts. 1. 2nd Colds. Gds.
Total.	–	–	5	6	
Other Divs.					
6th. City of London	–	1	2	–	
4th London Regt.	1	–	–	–	
Total.	1	1	2	[illegible]	

Prevailing Disease. – Nil.
No. with foot troubles – 1.

Evac'd by M.A.C.
Officers – Nil
Other Rks. 10
Ret'd to duty:–
Officers – 2
Other Rks. 2
Ret'd light duty –
Other Rks. 2

		Sick	Wndd.
Admitted	Officers.	1	1
"	Other Rks.	7	6
Evac'd	Officers	2	–
"	Other Rks.	11	4
Remng.	Officers.	7	3
"	Other Rks.	17	17

2nd Lt. J. G. GREGORY, 6th. City of London. Shell wnd. R. Thumb.
Lieut. A. B. LUCY, 4th London, Ventral Hernia.

P.A. Lloyd-Jones
Capt. RAMC.
O.C. No 4 Fd. Ambce.

A.D.M.S. 2nd Divn.
28/3/15.

No 4 Field Ambulance.

No of sick and wounded, by Units, admitted during 24 hours ended 9 am, 29/3/15

Unit. 2nd Divn.	Officers Sick	Officers Wnds.	Other Rks. Sick	Other Rks. Wnds.	Remarks.
2nd Gren. Gds.	–	–	2	1	
1st Irish Gds.	–	–	2	1	Duty.
1st Herts.	–	–	[illegible]	1	1. 1. Kings
1st R. Berks.	3	–	1	–	1. 1. K.R.R.
5th Kings.	[illegible]	–	2	–	1 RAMC.
9th H.L.I.	–	–	1	[illegible]	
A.S.C. 3 Coy.	–	–	1	–	
" 2 Div S. Col.	–	–	1	–	Light Duty.
R.F.A. (M.M.G.)	–	–	1	–	
" 2. D.A.C.	–	–	2	–	1 2nd Colds.
" 44 Bde.	–	–	1	–	1 4th R.W.F.
R.E. 5 Fd Co.	–	–	–	1	2. 2nd S. Staffs.
R.F.A. 17th Batt.	1	–	–	–	
RAMC.	1	–	–	–	
Total	5	–	14	4	
Other Divs.					
8th City of London.	–	–	1	1	
1st S.W.B.	–	1	–	–	
R.E. 35 Sig Co.	–	1	–	–	
1st Scots Gds.	1	–	–	–	
Total.	1	2	1	1	

Prevailing Disease Nil
No with foot troubles 1.

Evac. M.A.C.
Officers 3.
Other Rks. 11
Ret'd duty.
Officers Nil
Other Rks. 3.
Ret'd Lt. duty.
Other Rks. 4.

	Sick	Wnds.
Admitted Officers	6	2.
" Other Rks.	15	5
Evac' Officers	2	1
" Other Rks.	8	10
Remaining Officers	11	2.
" Other Rks.	18	11.

Capt. A.D. STRANGE, 1st R. Berks. Prom. Collateral.
2 Lt. W.J. COX, " " "
Lieut O.F. GREGORY, " " "
" B.M. GEE, R.F.A. 17 Batt. N.Y.D.
" H.D. WILLIS RAMC. Contusion Leg.
" E.P. ORR-EWING, 1st Scots Gds. I.C.T. Finger.
Capt. F.W. TOWNEND, R.E. 35 Sig Co., Shell wnds. Legs & R. Hand.
Lieut HARRY TRAVERS, 1st S.W.B. Bullet wnd Abdomen

A.D.M.S. 2nd Div.

P A Lloyd Jones.
Capt RAMC.
OC. No 4 Fd Amb.

No. 4 Field Ambulance.

No. of sick and wounded, by Units, admitted during 24 hours ended 9 am. 30/3/15.

Unit – 2nd Divn.	Officers Sick	Officers Wndd	Other Rks. Sick	Other Rks. Wndd.	Remarks.
2nd Grenadier Guards.	–	–	3	1.	
3rd Coldstream "	–	–	1	2	Officers to Duty
1st. Herts.	–	–	1	2	1 2nd Colds.
1st K.R.R.	1	–	–	–	
1/5th Kings.	–	–	1	–	To Light duty.
7th. Kings.	–	–	2	–	
2nd H. L. I.	–	–	1	–	1 2nd Gren Gds.
2nd R. Inniskg Fus.	–	–	–	2	1 113 Bat R F A.
R. F. A. 2nd D.A.C.	–	–	1	–	
R. G. A. 114 Batty	1	–	–	–	
" 56th "	–	–	1	–	
R.E. (Royal Anglesey)	1	–	–	–	
RAMC att. 2. Worcs.	–	1	–	–	
R. G. A. 7th M. Batt.	1	–	–	–	
Total.	4	1	11	7	
Other Divs.					
7th. City of London	–	–	1	1	
DAQMG. 1st. Divn.	1	–	–	–	
58th. Rifles	2	–	–	–	
3rd London	2	–	–	–	
5th London	–	–	–	2	
5th City of London	–	–	–	4	
Total.	5	–	1	7	

Prevailing Disease Nil.
No. with foot [illegible] Nil.

Evac. M.A.C.
Officers: 2.
Other Rks. ~~[illegible]~~ 13.
Ret'd duty
Officers 1.
Other Rks Nil
Ret'd Light duty
Other Rks ~~[illegible]~~ 2.

		Sick	Wndd
Admitted	Officers	9	1
"	Other Rks.	12	14
Evac'd	Officers	3	–
"	Other Rks	5	10
Remaining	Officers	7	3
"	Other Rks.	25	15.

Major J. M. YOUNG, D.A.Q.M.G. 1st Divn. Pharyngitis.
Lieut F. A. de V. ROBERTSON, 58th Rfls. [illegible].
Capt. G. S. BURN, " " [illegible].
Major. P. W. BERESFORD. 3rd London, Impetigo.
2nd Lt. F. C. DAVIS, " Catarrhal Jaundice.
Capt SL. J. R. RICHARDSON, 114 Batt. R. G. A. Influenza.
Major G. A. ARMITAGE, 1st. K. R. R. Internal derange't Knee Joint
Lieut. A. M. SMITH, RAMC (2nd Worcs) Shell wnd legs fractures.
Capt. R. WILLIAMS, R.E. (R. Anglesey) Frac. Thigh & Nose (accident).
Major B. A. M. HALL, R. G. A. 7th Mtn Batt. Influenza.

[illegible signature]
Capt. RAMC
OC. No 4 Fd Amb.

A.D.M.S. 2nd Divn.

No. 4 Field Ambulance.

No. of sick and wounded admitted, by units, during 24 hours ended 9 am. 31/3/15.

Unit – 2nd Divn.	Officers Sick	Officers Wndd	Other Rks. Sick	Other Rks. Wndd	Remarks.
2nd Grenadier Guards	–	–	1	2.	Duty.
2nd Coldstream	1	–	3	1	3. 8 City of London
1st Irish Guards	1	–	1	–	
1st Herts.	–	–	1	1	Lt. Duty.
1st R. Berks	–	–	1	–	1 RFA 50 Batt.
2nd S. Staffs.	–	–	1	–	1 5th Kings
7th Kings	1	–	1	–	1 1st K.R.R.
2nd R. Inniskg. Fus.	–	–	–	2	
R.F.A. 34th Bde.	–	–	1	–	
" (M. M. G. Sec.)	–	–	1	–	
R.G.A. 26th Hy Batt.	–	–	1	–	
RAMC No. 6 F.A.	–	–	1	–	
RFA 47 Batt.	1	–	–	–	
Total.	4	–	13	6	
Other Divns.					
4th R.W. Fus.	2	–	–	–	
1st L. N. Lancs.	1	–	–	–	
8th City of London	–	–	1	1	
1st S.W.B.	1	–	–	–	
I.M.S.	1	–	–	–	
Total.	5	–	1	1	

Prevailing disease Nil
No. with foot troubles Nil

Evac. M.A.C.
Officers 6 + 1 (2nd Div motor car).
Other Rks. 16.

Retd duty
Officers Nil
Other Rks. 3

Retd Lt. duty
Other Rks. 3

		Sick	Wndd
Admitted	Officers	9	–
"	Other Rks.	14	7.
Evac'd	Officers	6	–
"	Other Rks	15	7
Remaining	Officers	19	3
"	Other Rks.	24	15

Major W. R. WILSON, 4th R.W.F., Colic
Capt. T. O. BURY – do – Neurasthenia
2nd Lt. T. E. REDDING, 7th Kings Influenza.
Capt. F. N. GREENHILL 1st L. N. Lancs. Rheumatism
Lt. Sir J. M. WALKER, 2nd Colds. Influenza.
Lieut L. R. HARGREAVES, 1st Irish Gd. Ague.
Capt. LORD A. R. de FREYNE, 1st S.W.B. Influenza.
2nd Lt. H. CUTBUSH, R.F.A., 47 Batt. – do –
Capt. H. S. CORMACK, I.M.S. Influenza.

A.D.M.S. 2nd Divn.

[illegible]
Capt. RAMC.
OC. No. 4 Fd. Amb.

No. 4. 7. a. May 1915

Operations in March include :–

I For extraperitoneal wound of bladder

II Drainage of knee joint

III Amputation of Arm

IV Laparotomies. 2

V Depressed fracture of Skull = 4.

VI For fracture of legs = 2

BHG

www.ingramcontent.com/pod-product-compliance
Lightning Source LLC
Chambersburg PA
CBHW081426160426
43193CB00013B/2206

9781474503358